EASY ENGLISH

EASY ENGLISH

Basic English for Speakers of All Languages

Christopher A. Warnasch

ILLUSTRATIONS BY
Christopher Medellín

LIVING LANGUAGE®

Published in the United States by Living Language, an imprint of Random House, Inc.

www.livinglanguage.com

ISBN 978-1-4000-0604-5

Library of Congress Cataloging-in-Publication Data available upon request.

This book is available at special discounts for bulk purchases for sales promotions or premiums. Special editions, including personalized covers, excerpts of existing books, and corporate imprints, can be created in large quantities for special needs. For more information, write to Special Markets/Premium Sales, 1745 Broadway, MD 6-2, New York, New York 10019 or e-mail specialmarkets@randomhouse.com.

PRINTED IN THE UNITED STATES OF AMERICA

10   9   8   7   6   5   4   3

CONTENTS

Contents

Contents

ALPHABET

 Aa Bb Cc Dd Ee Ff Gg Hh Ii Jj Kk
Ll Mm Nn Oo Pp Qq Rr Ss Tt Uu
Vv Ww Xx Yy Zz

PRONUNCIATION

A	am, at, an, add, ask, bad, cab, chat, dab, fax, gas, has, jar, lab, man, nag, pass, rat, sat, sham, tap, that, vat, wax, yak, zag
E	ebb, Ed, bed, check, den, fell, get, help, Jen, kept, less, men, nest, pen, quest, rent, set, shell, ten, them, vet, went, yes, Zed
I	is, in, ill, big, chick, dig, film, gift, his, kill, lift, mix, nick, pit, quiz, rim, sit, shift, tick, this, thick, Vic, will, zip
O	on, ox, opt, Bob, cog, chop, dock, fox, got, hop, job, Koch, lock, mop, not, pop, rock, sock, shot, Tom, thong, wok
U	up, us, bus, cup, chunk, duck, fun, Gus, hum, just, luck, must, nut, puff, rust, sun, shut, tug, thumb, yuck
U	bull, full, put, pull
A-E	ate, ale, ape, babe, cave, chase, daze, fake,

game, hate, jade, kale, lame, made, name, paste, quake, rake, sane, shake, tame, vase, wake

AI	ail, bail, fail, hail, mail, pail, quail, rail
AY	bay, day, hay, Jay, May, pay, ray, say, way
AU	taught, caught, auto, Austin, Maud
AW	maw, claw, paw, draw, saw
E-E	eve, here, Pete
EE	eel, beet, cheese, deep, feel, geese, jeep, keep, Lee, meet, need, peer, queen, seem, tree, thee, week
EA	east, ear, eat, beast, dean, fear, gear, heat, lean, mean, pea, read, seat, tea, year, zeal
EW	blew, chew, dew, few, grew, mew, new, pew
I-E	ire, Ike, ile, bike, chime, dime, fine, hide, like, Mike, nice, pike, ripe, size, shine, time, vine, wine
IGH	bight, fight, fright, high, light, might, night, right, sigh, sight, tight, thigh
IE	die, lie, pie, tie
O-E	ode, owe, bode, code, dome, home, joke, lone, mope, note, poke, rope, soke, shone, tone, vote, woke, yoke, zone
OA	oat, oaf, boat, coat, foam, goal, hoax, load, moan, roam, soap

OI	foil, join, joint, boil, noise
OY	boy, coy, toy, Roy, joy
OU	loud, proud, sound, bound, mound
OW	down, gown, brow, cow, clown, now
OW	grow, mow, blow, know, glow
OO	ooze, boom, coop, choose, doom, food, goose, hoop, loose, moose, noon, soon, tooth, zoom
OO	book, cook, hook, hood, look, nook, soot, took, wool, wood
U-E	use, dude, fume, huge, luge, rude, mule, plume, tune, tube
UE	blue, fuel, glue, hue, Sue, true
Y-E	byte, type, hype, rye, dye
Y	by, cry, dry, fry, my, pry, shy, why
Y	Betty, dolly, fully, gully, happy, hilly, jelly, Kelly, Molly
B	bag, bake, beg, bib, boom
C	cake, coat, cap, can, cup, cook
CK	sock, sick, pick, luck, lick
CH	chair, choose, chew, chime, China
D	dog, dome, do, Dad, day
F	fake, fan, fix, fine, food
G	go, gave, game, get, gag

G	gin, gem, gist, gel, Giles
H	hi, hope, hop, high, hail
J	Jake, joke, job, jail, John
K	king, kiss, kid, kind, koala
L	load, lobe, log, last, light
M	man, mom, moan, might, Mike
N	not, name, Nile, nick, nest
P	pack, pole, pool, pin, pine
PH	photo, phone
QU	quack, quake, queen, quail, quit
R	rust, room, ripe, right, rent
S	Sam, sit, sank, sight, send, sift
SH	she, show, shell, shin, shine
T	ten, tight, tuft, tip, tame
TH	they, though, then, that, there
TH	with, through, think, bath, Seth
V	Vic, vine, vat, vase, veer
W	week, wig, wine, wag, we
WH	who, what, where, when, why
X	ox, axe, six, tax, fox
Y	year, you, yell, yen, Yale
Z	zen, zoo, zoom, zigzag, Zed

EASY ENGLISH

L E S S O N   1
Hello!

👉 **WORD STUDY**

Hello!   Hi!

How are you?      I'm fine,
                                                 thanks.

How are you?   Very good!

🗫 **DIALOGUE**

🎧 *Mr. Peterson:* **Hello, Mrs.
    Ramirez.**
Mrs. Ramirez: **Hello, Mr.
    Peterson. How are you?**
Mr. Peterson: **I'm fine, thank you. And you?**
Mrs. Ramirez: **Fine, thank you.**

Hiroko: **Hello.**
Maria: **Hello! I'm Maria
    Sandoval. What's your name?**
Hiroko: **My name is Hiroko
    Yamada.**
Maria: **How are you?**

Hiroko: **I'm fine, thank you. And you?**
Maria: **Fine, thanks. It's nice to meet you, Hiroko.**
Hiroko: **It's nice to meet you, too.**

François: **Hi, John.**
John: **Hey, François. How are you?**
François: **Good. And you?**
John: **Good.**

VOCABULARY

Hello.	**Thanks.**
Hi.	**name**
Hey.	**my**
I	**your**
you	**what**
fine	**nice**
good	**too**
very good	**What's your name?**
How are you?	**My name is John.**
I'm fine.	**It's nice to meet**
Thank you.	**you.**

STRUCTURE

1. I am, you are

I am.
I am John Cooper.

I am.
I am Maria Sandoval.

You are.
You are Maria Sandoval.

2. You are . . . Are you . . . ?

Are you Maria?

3. Yes / No

John: Are you Natasha?
Maria: No, I'm Maria.
John: Are you Maria?
Maria: Yes, I'm Maria.

4. I am, I am not (I'm, I'm not)

Natasha: Are you John?
François: No, I am not John.
Natasha: Are you Ram?

François: No, I'm not Ram.
Natasha: Are you François?
François: Yes, I'm François.

EXERCISES

A. *Mr. Yamada:* Hello, Mr. Peterson.

Mr. Peterson: _____. Are _____

Mr. Yamada?

Mr. Yamada: Yes, I _____.

Mr. Peterson: It's _____ to

_____ you.

Mr. Yamada: It's _____ to

_____ you, _____.

B. *Maria:* My _____ is Maria Sandoval.

What's _____ name?

Natasha: _____ name is Natasha

Ivanovna.

Maria: How _____ _____,

Natasha?

Natasha: _____ fine, thanks. And

_____?

Maria: I'm fine.

C. am, are, is

1. I _____ Maria.

2. How _____ you?

3. _____ you Natasha Ivanova?

4. My name _____ Ram.

5. _____ you John? Yes, I

_____ .

D. You are Maria.

Are you Maria?

1. You are Natasha.

_____.

2. You are Mr. Smith.

_____.

3. You are Mrs. Martinez.

_____.

4. You are John.

_____.

A. Hello, you, am, nice, meet, nice, meet, too

B. name, your, My, are, you, I'm, you

C. 1. am, 2. are, 3. Are, 4. is, 5. Are, am

*D. 1. Are you Natasha? 2. Are you Mr. Smith?
3. Are you Mrs. Martinez? 4. Are you John?*

WORD STUDY

This is François Laret.

François is from Haiti.

He is not American. He is Haitian.

This is Hiroko Yamada.

Hiroko is from Japan.

She is not American.
She is Japanese.

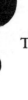

This is Maria. Where is Maria from?

Maria is from Mexico.
She is Mexican.

DIALOGUE

John: **Ram, this is Natasha.**

Ram: **Hello, Natasha. It's nice to meet you.**

Natasha: **Hello, Ram. It's nice to meet you, too.**

Ram: **Natasha is a Russian name. Are you from Russia?**

Natasha: **Yes, I am. I'm from Moscow. Where are you from, Ram?**

Ram: **I'm from India. Ram is an Indian name.**

John: **Yes, Ram is Indian. He's from Mumbai.**

VOCABULARY

this	Japanese	you
from	Russian	she
where	Mexican	he
and	am	we
American	are	they
Haitian	is	not
Indian	I	

8

STRUCTURE

1. I am, you are, he is, she is, we are, they are

I am John.

You are Maria.

He is Ram.

She is Natasha.

We are John, Ram, and Natasha.

You are Ram and Natasha.

They are Ram and Natasha.

2. American, Indian, Mexican ...

This is Maria. She is from Mexico.
She is Mexican.

This is Hiroko.
She is from Japan.
She is Japanese.

This is François. He is from Haiti.
He is Haitian.

This is John. He is from the USA. He is
American.

This is Ram. He is from India. He is Indian.

This is Natasha. She is from Russia. She is
Russian.

3. Not

This is not Hiroko. This
is not François. This is
Natasha.

Natasha is not Japanese.
Natasha is not Haitian.
She is Russian.

4. I'm, you're, he's . . .

I am John. I'm John. I'm from New York. I'm not Russian. I'm American.

You are Maria. = You're Maria. You're from Mexico. You're not from India.

He is Ram. = He's Ram. He's from India. He's not American.

He is John. = He's John. He's from New York. He's not from Mumbai.

We are Hiroko and Kenji. = We're Hiroko and Kenji. We're from Japan. We're Japanese. We're not from India. We're not Indian.

You are Ram and Natasha. = You're Ram and Natasha. You're not Maria and François.

They are Ram and Natasha. = They're Ram and Amrita. They're from Mumbai. They're Indian. They're not Haitian. They're not from Port-au-Prince.

EXERCISES

A. am, are, is

1. I _____ John.
2. He _____ from India.
3. She _____ not from New York.
4. _____ you American?
5. This _____ Ram.
6. We _____ John, Ram, and Natasha.
7. They _____ not from Mexico.
8. _____ this Maria?

B. 1. John is from the USA. He is _____.

2. Ram is from India. He is _____.
3. Maria is from Mexico. She is _____.
4. Hiroko is from Japan. She is _____.
5. François is from Haiti. He is _____.
6. Natasha is from Russia.

   She is _____.

C. Ram / from India.
Ram is from India.

Ram / Haitian.
Ram is not Haitian.

1. Natasha / from New York.

   _____.

2. Maria / from Mexico.

   _____.

3. John / from Japan.

   _____.

4. François / Russian.

   _____.

5. Hiroko / from India.

   _____.

6. Ram / Indian.

   _____.

D. I am John.
I'm John.

1. You are from Japan.

   _____.

2. He is not American.

   _____.

3. I am Indian.

   _____.

4. We are not from Mexico. We are from New York.

   _____.

5. They are Ram and Amrita. They are from Mumbai.

   _____.

6. She is Japanese. She is not Indian.

   _____.

A. 1. *am*, 2. *is*, 3. *is*, 4. *Are*, 5. *is*, 6. *are*, 7. *are*, 8. *Is*

B. 1. *American*, 2. *Indian*, 3. *Mexican*, 4. *Japanese*, 5. *Haitian*, 6. *Russian*

C. 1. *Natasha is not from New York.* 2. *Maria is from Mexico.* 3. *John is not from Japan.* 4. *François is not Russian.* 5. *Hiroko is not from India.* 6. *Ram is Indian.*

D. 1. *You're from Japan.* 2. *He's not American.* 3. *I'm Indian.* 4. *We're not from Mexico. We're from New York.* 5. *They're Ram and Amrita. They're from Mumbai.* 6. *She's Japanese. She's not Indian.*

LESSON 3
What's This?

This is a book.

This is a car.

This isn't a book.
This isn't a car. This is a
computer.

I have a computer.

I have a book.

I have a car.

What's this?

15

old

new

good

bad

  DIALOGUE

Maria: **François, what's this?**

François: **It's a computer.**

Maria: **Is it new?**

François: **Yes, it is.**

Maria: **I have a computer in the office.**

François: **Is it a good computer?**

Maria: **No, it's a bad computer. It's old.**

VOCABULARY

book	computer	new
car	old	good

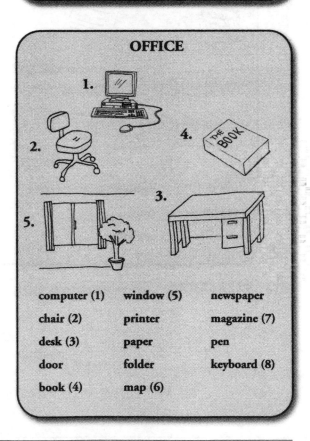

OFFICE

computer (1)	window (5)	newspaper
chair (2)	printer	magazine (7)
desk (3)	paper	pen
door	folder	keyboard (8)
book (4)	map (6)	

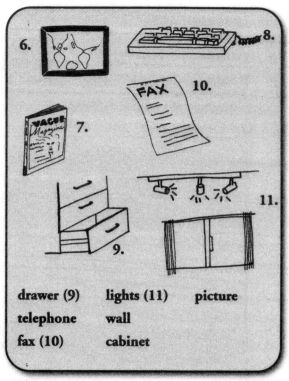

drawer (9)	lights (11)	picture
telephone	wall	
fax (10)	cabinet	

STRUCTURE

1. It

This is a car. It's new.
It's a good car.

This isn't a picture. It's a book.

Is this a magazine? No, it's not a magazine. It's a computer.

2. I have, you have, he has . . .

Ram has a computer.   Maria has a book.

John has a new car.

<u>I have</u> a new book.

<u>You have</u> a new car.

<u>He has</u> a magazine.

<u>She has</u> a cup.

<u>We have</u> a newspaper.

<u>They have</u> a map.

3. In

This is a pen. It is in a cup.

Maria has a computer in the office.

Tokyo is in Japan. Moscow is in Russia.

Mumbai is in India.

The Statue of Liberty and the Brooklyn Bridge are in New York.

EXERCISES

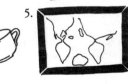

A. *This is a computer.*

1. _____

2. _____

3. _____

4. _____

5. _____

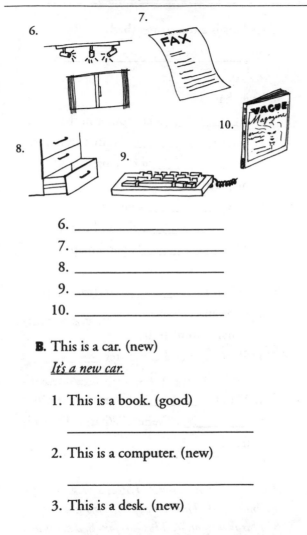

6. _____

7. _____

8. _____

9. _____

10. _____

B. This is a car. (new)
   It's a new car.

1. This is a book. (good)

   _____

2. This is a computer. (new)

   _____

3. This is a desk. (new)

   _____

4. This is a magazine. (bad)

_____

C. have, has

1. I _____ a computer in the office.
2. Natasha _____ a Russian name.
3. We _____ a newspaper and a magazine.
4. You _____ a new car.
5. He _____ a pen and paper.
6. They _____ a good map.

D. 1. Tokyo is _____ (in/from) Japan.
2. Ram and Amrita are _____ (where/from) India.
3. She has a good computer _____ (from/in) the office.
4. Maria _____ (is/are) in the office.
5. _____ (Where/What) is François from?

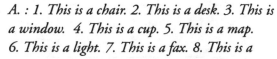

A. : 1. This is a chair. 2. This is a desk. 3. This is a window. 4. This is a cup. 5. This is a map. 6. This is a light. 7. This is a fax. 8. This is a *drawer. 9. This is a keyboard. 10. This is a magazine.*

B. 1. It's a good book. 2. It's a new computer. 3. It's a new desk. 4. It's a bad magazine.

C. 1. have, 2. has, 3. have, 4. have, 5. has, 6. have

D. 1. in, 2. from, 3. in, 4. is, 5. Where

Welcome to My House!

 **WORD STUDY**

This is a house.
This is a big house.

This is a house.
This is a little house.

This is a house.
This is a very big house.

This is a beautiful house,

and this is an ugly house.

1 - one   2 - two   3 - three   4 - four   5 - five

This is a book.   These are three books.

There is a book   There are three books
on the table.   on the table.

These are dogs.   These are black dogs.

I have a big dog. My dog is big.

You have a little dog.
Your dog is little.

Please, come in!

Please, sit down!

🎧 DIALOGUE

Hiroko: **Ram, Natasha, hello! Welcome!**
Ram: **Hello, Hiroko!**
Natasha: **Hi, Hiroko. How are you?**
Hiroko: **I'm fine, thanks. Please come in!**
Natasha: **Your house is very beautiful.**
Ram: **Yes, Hiroko. You have a beautiful house.**
Hiroko: **This is the living room. There's a big**

kitchen, there are three bedrooms, and
there are two bathrooms.

Ram: Is there a dining room?

Hiroko: Yes, there's a dining room, too.

Natasha: Is the dining room big or small?

Hiroko: The dining room is small.

Ram: It's very beautiful.

Hiroko: Thank you! Please, sit down!

VOCABULARY

house	two
big	three
little	four
very	five
beautiful	too
ugly	on
one	

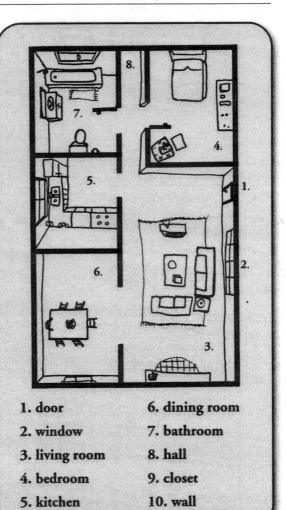

1. door
2. window
3. living room
4. bedroom
5. kitchen

6. dining room
7. bathroom
8. hall
9. closet
10. wall

LIVING ROOM

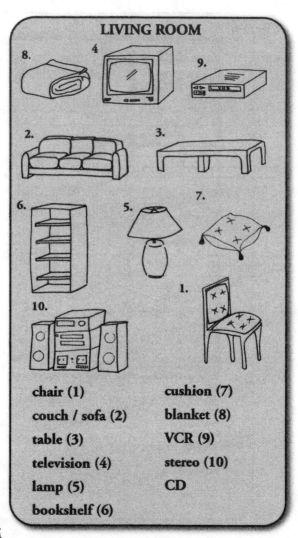

chair (1)	cushion (7)
couch / sofa (2)	blanket (8)
table (3)	VCR (9)
television (4)	stereo (10)
lamp (5)	CD
bookshelf (6)	

STRUCTURE

1. book / books

a book   books

a cup   cups

Ram has a computer.   Natasha has two computers.

This is a big bedroom.   Hiroko has three big bedrooms.

This is a black dog.   These are black dogs.

2. There is (There's) / There are

There's one book on the table.   There are three books on the table.

There's a big kitchen in the house.

There are three bedrooms in the house.

There are two chairs and a couch in the living room.

Is there a bed in the bedroom?	Yes, there's a bed in the bedroom.
Is there a VCR in the living room?	Yes, there's a VCR in the living room.
Are there books on the bookshelf?	Yes, there are books on the bookshelf.

3. a / an

<u>A</u> + b, c, d, f, g, h, j, k, l, m, n, p, qu, r, s, t, v, w, x, y, z

This is <u>a</u> computer.

Hiroko has <u>a</u> television.

There is <u>a</u> window in the office.

John has <u>a</u> new car.

<u>AN</u> + a, e, i, o, u

This is <u>an</u> old car.

John has <u>an</u> office.

This is <u>an</u> ugly house.

4. This is / These are

book	books
This is a book.	These are books.
This is a car.	These are cars.
This is a good magazine.	These are good magazines.
This is an old computer.	These are old computers.
This is an office.	These are offices.

5. the

This is a tower.

The Eiffel Tower is in Paris.

This is a flag.

This is the Japanese flag.

This is the American flag.

This is a statue.

The Statue of Liberty is in New York.

<u>a</u> dog

John has <u>a</u> dog.

<u>the</u> dog

<u>The</u> dog is big and black.

6. in, on

There is a book on the table.	There are three books on the table.
The book is on the table.	The table is in the house.
There are cushions on the couch.	The couch is in the living room.
The Brooklyn Bridge is in New York.	There are cars on the bridge.
The map is in the office.	The map is on the wall.

 EXERCISES

A. This is a book.

These are books.

1. This is a house.

_____

2. This is an office.

   _____

3. This is a pen.

   _____

4. This is a kitchen.

   _____

5. This is a big dog.

   _____

6. This is a new car.

   _____

B. There is, There are

1. _____ a table in the living room.

2. _____ chairs in the living room.

3. _____ a lamp in the living room.

4. _____ a television in the living room.

5. _____ a couch in the
   living room.

6. _____ books in the
   living room.

C. a, an

1. This is _____ new car.
2. John has _____ old computer.
3. Hiroko and Kenji have _____
   beautiful house.
4. This is _____ office.
5. This is _____ beautiful picture, and
   this is _____ ugly picture.

D. the, a, an

1. This is _____ beautiful bridge.
2. _____ Brooklyn Bridge is very big.
3. Where is _____ Statue of Liberty?
4. Is there _____ desk in the office?
5. Is this _____ Mexican flag?
6. Ram has _____ old car.
7. _____ car is black.
8. Maria has _____ black car, too.

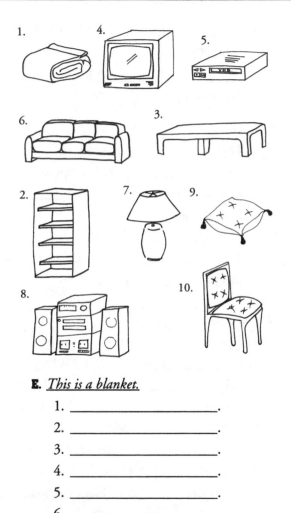

E. *This is a blanket.*

1. _____.
2. _____.
3. _____.
4. _____.
5. _____.
6. _____.
7. _____.

8. _____.

9. _____.

10. _____.

F. 1. There is a pen (in/on) _____ the desk.

2. They have a computer (in/on) _____ the living room.

3. Chicago is (in/on) _____ Illinois.

4. The map is (in/on) _____ the wall.

5. Maria has the file (in/on) _____ the drawer.

6. The books are (in/on) _____ the bookshelf.

7. There is a blanket (in/on) _____ the bed.

8. My CDs are (in/on) _____ my bedroom.

A. 1. These are houses. 2. These are offices. 3. These are pens. 4. These are kitchens. 5. These are big dogs. 6. These are new cars.

B. 1. There is, 2. There are, 3. There is, 4. There is, 5. There is, 6. There are

C. 1. a, 2. an, 3. a, 4. an, 5. a, an

D. 1. a, 2. The, 3. the, 4. a, 5. the, 6. an, 7. The, 8. a

E. 1. This is a blanket. 2. This is a bookshelf. 3. This is a table. 4. This is a television. 5. This is a VCR. 6. This is a couch. / This is a sofa. 7. This is a lamp. 8. This is a stereo. 9. This is a cushion. 10. This is a chair.

F. 1. on, 2. in, 3. in, 4. on, 5. in, 6. on, 7. on, 8. in

L E S S O N   5
Is This Your Disk?

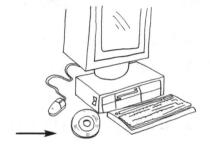

This is a disk.   The disk is on the desk, next to the computer.

The keyboard is in front of the computer.

This is an empty cup, and this is a full cup.

This is Ram's computer, and this is Maria's book.

Is it Ram's car?   No, it's not.

Is it Maria's car?   No, it's not.

Whose car is it?   It's John's car.

She is tall, and he is short.

She has long hair, and he has short hair.

DIALOGUE

Maria: Peter, is this disk next to the computer full?

Peter: It's not my disk.

Maria: Whose disk is it?

Peter: It's Janet's. She's the tall woman with the long hair. She's in front of the window.

Maria: Janet, is this your disk?

Janet: Yes, it is. But it's old.

Maria: Is it full?

Janet: Yes.

Maria: Do you have a new disk?

Janet: Here. Have this one. It's empty.

Maria: Thanks.

VOCABULARY

next to	tall	knife
in front of	short	spoon
empty	long	plate
full	short	napkin
whose?	fork	cup

The knife and spoon are on the napkin.

The fork is next to the plate.

The knife and spoon are on the right.

The fork is on the left.

The plate is between the fork and the knife.

The glass is in front of the plate.

The cup is across from the glass.

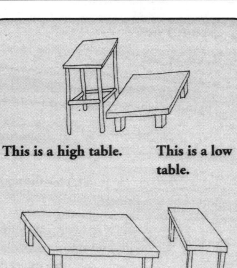

This is a high table.   **This is a low table.**

This is a wide table.   **This is a narrow table.**

Hiroko is happy.   **Maria is thin.**
She is sad.   **She is fat.**

STRUCTURE

1. am, is, are

I am John. I am American. I'm from New York.
I'm not tall, but I'm not short.

You are Natasha. You are not from America.
You're Russian. You're beautiful.

He is François. He is tall. He's from Haiti. He's
from Port-au-Prince.

She is Hiroko. She's Japanese. She's from
Tokyo. She's short and thin.

We are Ram and Amrita. We're not from the
USA. We're from India. We're Indian.

They are Maria and Jose. They're from Mexico.
They're Mexican.

2. a, an, the

This is <u>a</u> computer. <u>The</u> computer is new. <u>The</u>
computer is on <u>the</u> desk.

This is <u>a</u> keyboard. <u>The</u> keyboard is in front of
<u>the</u> computer.

This is <u>an</u> office. <u>The</u> office is not big, and it's
not small.

This is <u>an</u> old house, and this is <u>an</u> ugly car.

There is <u>an</u> empty cup on <u>the</u> table.

3. Is the . . . ?

The keyboard is in front of the computer.	Is the keyboard in front of the computer?
The fork is on the left.	Is the fork on the left?
The spoon and knife are on the right.	Are the spoon and knife on the right?
Mumbai is far from New York.	Is Mumbai far from New York?

4. window, windows . . .

This is a table.	These are tables.
You have a magazine.	He has magazines.
They have an ugly car.	We have new cars.

EXERCISES

A. am, are, is

1. I _____ from Mumbai.

2. They _____ not in New York.

3. We _____ in the car, and you

   _____ next to it.

4. _____ you in the living room or the dining room?

5. _____ your kitchen big or small?

6. Where _____ the bathroom?

7. John, François, and Ram _____ not happy.

8. You _____ in the office.

B. old/new, big/small . . .

1. François isn't short, he's _____.

2. Ram's computer isn't new, it's

   _____.

3. This isn't a _____ dog, it's a good dog!

4. My house isn't ugly, it's _____.

5. The table next to the couch isn't high, it's

   _____.

6. Your office isn't _____, it's wide.

7. She's not happy, she's _____.

8. New York isn't _____, it's big.

9. My cup isn't full, it's _____.

10. The children aren't _____, they're thin.

11. Your hair isn't _____, it's long.

12. The fork isn't on the right, it's on the

    _____.

C. The bedrooms in this house are big.
Are the bedrooms in this house big?

1. The pens and pencils are in the drawer.

   _____.

2. François is from Haiti.

   _____.

3. The house is very beautiful.

   _____.

4. It's far from my house.

   _____.

5. There are three empty offices.

   _____.

6. The Brooklyn Bridge and the Empire State
   Building are in New York.

   _____.

D. 1. There (is/are) _____ three big bedrooms in the house.
2. (Is/Are) _____ there an empty
   office?
3. There (is/are) _____ an old Russian
   book on the table.

4. (Is/Are) _____ there pens and pencils in the drawer?

5. There (is/are) _____ one window in the bathroom.

6. There (is/are) _____ four new disks on my desk.

E. 1. He (has/have) _____ a very big office.

2. They (has/have) _____ empty glasses.

3. I (has/have) _____ a good dog.

4. You (has/have) _____ the files in your drawer.

5. She (has/have) _____ my CDs in the car.

6. We (has/have) _____ a new stereo and VCR.

A. 1.am, 2. are, 3. are, are, 4. Are, 5. Is, 6. is, 7. are, are

B. 1. tall, 2. old, 3. bad, 4. beautiful, 5. low, 6. narrow, 7. sad, 8. small, 9. empty, 10. fat, 11. short, 12. left

C. 1. Are the pens and pencils in the drawer? 2. Is

François from Haiti? 3. Is the house very beautiful? 4. Is it far from my house? 5. Are there three empty offices? 6. Are the Brooklyn Bridge and the Empire State Building in New York?

D. 1. are, 2. Is, 3. is, 4. Are, 5. is, 6. are

E. 1. has, 2. have, 3. have, 4. have, 5. has, 6. have

L E S S O N   6
Who's That?

 WORD STUDY

This is Natasha.　　That is Ram.

This is a man and　　That is a boy and that
this is a woman.　　is a girl.

Who is this?

Ram is in the car,
and John is next
to the car.

These are children. There are three boys and four girls.

DIALOGUE

Maria: **Natasha, who's that?**

Natasha: **Who? The woman in the car?**

Maria: **No, the man next to Hiroko.**

Natasha: **The man next to Hiroko? That's Kenji.**

Maria: **Who's Kenji?**

Natasha: **Kenji is Hiroko's husband.**

Maria: **And who are the children next to Hiroko and Kenji?**

Natasha: **The girl is Chikako and the boy is**

Akira. Chikako is Kenji's and Hiroko's daughter, and Akira is Kenji's and Hiroko's son.

VOCABULARY

this	who	next to
that	in	children
these		

man   woman   boy girl

family

father   daughter

mother   son

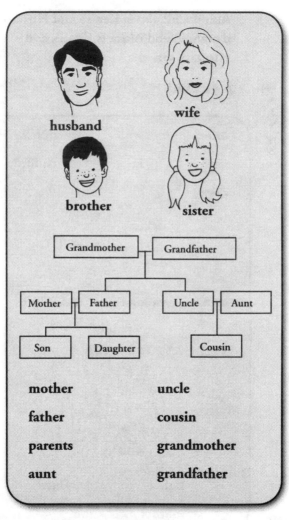

husband

wife

brother

sister

| Grandmother | Grandfather |

| Mother | Father | | Uncle | Aunt |

| Son | Daughter | | | Cousin |

mother

father

parents

aunt

uncle

cousin

grandmother

grandfather

STRUCTURE

1. Who?

Who's this?

Who's this?   It's John.

Who's this?	It's Natasha.
And who's that?	It's Ram.
Who's Hiroko's husband?	Kenji is Hiroko's husband.

2. This is . . . / That is . . .

These are . . . / Those are . . .

This is Natasha.	That is Ram.
This is a computer.	That is a book.

These are computers.

Those are books.

This is the Mexican flag.

That is the American flag.

These are flags.

Those are flags, too.

3. Hiroko's, John's

Hiroko has a beautiful house.

Hiroko's house is beautiful.

John has a black dog.

John's dog is black.

Kenji has a wife.

Hiroko is Kenji's wife.

François has a new computer.

François's computer is new.

 EXERCISES

A. 1. This is a _____.
     2. This is a _____.
     3. This is a _____.
     4. This is a _____.

B. 1. Hiroko is Kenji's _____
   (husband/wife).

2. Kenji is Akira's _____
   (son/father).

3. Chikako is Akira's _____
   (daughter/sister).

4. Akira is Chikako's _____
   (brother/sister).

5. Hiroko is Chikako's and Akira's
   _____ (mother/father)

6. Kenji's and Hiroko's (daughter/son)
   _____ is Chikako.

C. Who is from the USA, John or Kenji?
   John is from the USA.

1. Who is Akira's father, François or Kenji?

   _____.

2. Who is from India, Ram or John?

   _____.

3. Who is Ram's wife, Hiroko or Amrita?

   _____.

4. Who is Chikako's brother, Akira or Ram?

   _____.

D. 1. (This/That) _____ is Ram.

2. (This/That) _____ is Natasha.

3. (This/That) _____ is John.

4. (This/That) _____ is a man.

5. (This/That) _____ is a woman.

6. (This/That) _____ is a girl, and
   (this/that) _____ is a boy.

E. John has a black dog.
John's dog is black.

1. Hiroko has a big house.

   _____.

2. Maria has a new computer.

   _____.

3. Ram has an old car.

   _____.

4. Hiroko has a Japanese husband.

   _____.

5. John has a little office.

   _____.

6. Natasha has a Russian newspaper.

   _____.

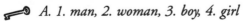 *A. 1. man, 2. woman, 3. boy, 4. girl*

*B. 1. wife, 2. father, 3. sister, 4. brother,
5. mother, 6. daughter*

*C. 1. Kenji is Akira's father. 2. Ram is from India.
3. Amrita is Ram's wife. 4. Akira is Chikako's
brother.*

D. 1. That is Ram. 2. This is Natasha. 3. This is John. 4. This is a man. 5. This is a woman. 6. That is a girl, and that is a boy.

E. 1. Hiroko's house is big. 2. Maria's computer is new. 3. Ram's car is old. 4. Hiroko's husband is Japanese. 5. John's office is little. 6. Natasha's newspaper is Russian.

What Number Is This?

WORD STUDY

1	2	3	4	5
one	two	three	four	five
6	7	8	9	10
six	seven	eight	nine	ten

3, 6, 4, 10, 2

These are numbers.

$$4 + 4 = 8$$

right

$$4 + 4 = 6$$

wrong

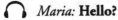

DIALOGUE

Maria: **Hello?**

Voice: **Hello, is this Laura Jackson?**

Maria: **No, it's not.**

Voice: **Is this 555-2347?**

Maria: **No, it's not. This is 555-2348.**

Voice: **Oh, do I have the wrong number?**
Maria: **Yes, you do.**
Voice: **I'm sorry.**
Maria: **That's okay. Good-bye.**
Voice: **Good-bye.**

VOCABULARY

number	numbers
right	wrong
0 zero	10 ten
1 one	11 eleven
2 two	12 twelve
3 three	13 thirteen
4 four	14 fourteen
5 five	15 fifteen
6 six	16 sixteen
7 seven	17 seventeen
8 eight	18 eighteen
9 nine	19 nineteen
	20 twenty

STRUCTURE

1. Yes, it is. / No, it's not.

Is this John?	Yes, it is.
Is this Natasha?	No, it's not.

Is this an old car?	Yes, it is.
Is this a new car?	No, it's not.
Is that a new computer?	Yes, it is.
Is that an old car?	No, it's not.
Is Kenji Hiroko's husband?	Yes, he is.
Is Kenji Hiroko's son?	No, he's not.
Is Hiroko Chikako's mother?	Yes, she is.
Is Chikako Natasha's daughter?	No, she's not.
Are Kenji and Hiroko Japanese?	Yes, they are.

Are Amrita and Ram
Japanese?

No, they're not.

2. doesn't have / don't have

Ram has a computer.

Ram doesn't
have a book

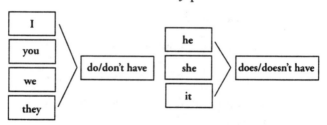

Maria has a book.

She doesn't
have a newspaper.

John has an American
car.

He doesn't have a
Japanese car.

I you we they	do/don't have	he she it	does/doesn't have

I have the wrong
number.

I don't have the wrong
the number.

You have two children.

You don't have two
children.

John has a big dog.

John doesn't have
a big dog.

Maria has a good
book.

Maria doesn't have a
good book.

We have a magazine.	We don't have a magazine.
They have a big dining room.	They don't have a big dining room.

3. Do / Does . . . have?

Does Natasha have a big dog?	Yes, she does.
Does she have a little dog?	No, she doesn't.
Does François have a book?	Yes, he does.
Does François have a computer?	No, he doesn't.
Does Ram have a newspaper?	Yes, he does.
Does he have a book?	No, he doesn't

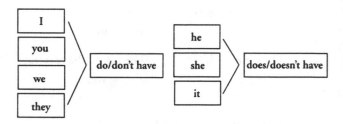

Do I have the wrong number?	Yes, you do.
Do I have the right number?	No, you don't.
Do you have two children?	Yes, I do.
Do you have three children?	No, I don't.
Does John have a big dog?	Yes, he does.
Does John have a little dog?	No, he doesn't.
Does Maria have a good book?	Yes, she does.
Does Maria have a bad book?	No, she doesn't.
Do we have a magazine?	Yes, we do.

Do we have a newspaper?	No, we don't.
Do they have a big dining room?	Yes, they do.
Do they have a big kitchen?	No, they don't.

EXERCISES

A. Are we in New York? (Yes)

Yes, we are.

1. Are we in a Japanese car? (No)

   _____.

2. Is John American? (Yes)

   _____.

3. Are Amrita and Ram from Russia? (No)

   _____.

4. Am I right? (Yes, I . . .)

   _____.

5. Are you at the office? (Yes, you . . .)

   _____.

6. Is Natasha from Mexico? (No)

   _____.

7. Is this a good book? (Yes)

   _____.

8. Is that a new computer? (No)

   _____.

B. 1. Ram (doesn't/don't) _____ have a son.

2. Akira and Chikako (doesn't/don't) _____ have big bedrooms.

3. John (doesn't/don't) _____ have a big car.

4. I (doesn't/don't) _____ have a dog.

5. She (doesn't/don't) _____ have the right number.

6. We (doesn't/don't) _____ have paper and pens.

7. They (doesn't/don't) _____ have a beautiful house.

8. Natasha (doesn't/don't) _____ have a good computer.

C. Do / Don't / Does / Doesn't

   _____ Akira have a big bedroom? No, he _____.

Does Akira have a big bedroom? No, he doesn't.

1. _____ Chikako have a brother? Yes, she _____.

2. _____ Ram and Amrita have children? No, they _____.

3. _____ John have a big office? No, he _____.

4. _____ Natasha and Maria have good books? Yes, they _____.

5. _____ I have a nice house? Yes, I _____.

6. _____ we have an American car? No, we _____.

D. 1. Three and four are _____.

2. Eleven and _____ are thirteen.

3. Five and twelve are _____.

4. _____ and six are nineteen.

5. One and _____ are seven.

6. _____ and eight are eighteen.

7. Five and three are _____.

8. Two and two are _____.

A. 1.No, we aren't. (No, we're not.) 2. Yes, he is.
3. No, they aren't. (No they're not.) 4. Yes, I am.
5. Yes, you are. 6. No, she isn't. (No, she's not.)
7. Yes, it is. 8. No, it's not. (No, it isn't.)

B. 1. doesn't, 2. don't, 3. doesn't, 4. don't,
5. doesn't, 6. don't, 7. don't, 8. doesn't

C. 1. Does, does, 2. Do, don't (do not), 3. Does,
doesn't (does not.), 4. Do, do, 5. Do, do, 6. Do,
don't (do not)

D. 1. seven, 2. two, 3. seventeen, 4. Thirteen, 5.
six, 6. Ten, 7. eight, 8. four

L E S S O N   8
Is the Post Office Open Today?

 WORD STUDY

These are days.

Monday	Friday
Tuesday	Saturday
Wednesday	Sunday
Thursday	

Today is Tuesday.

This is a post office.

These are stamps.

This is a bank.

73

open   closed

❄ DIALOGUE

John: Hi, Ram. How
   are you today?
Ram: Hi, John. I'm
   fine, thanks.
John: Where's Amrita?
Ram: She's at the store.
   John, is the post office open today? I don't
   have any stamps.
John: Today's Tuesday. The post office is open
   on Tuesday.
Ram: Is the bank open today?
John: Yes, it is. The bank is closed Sundays,
   but it's open today.
Ram: Where is the bank?
John: It's next to the police station. They're
   on Second Street.

VOCABULARY

day	parking lot
Sunday	today
Monday	post office
Tuesday	stamps
Wednesday	bank
Thursday	open
Friday	closed
Saturday	police station
town	newspaper stand
bank	gas station
post office	firehouse
library	church
school	restaurant
(food) store	hotel
supermarket	hospital
shoe store	train station
bookstore	bus stop
street	park
sidewalk	

STRUCTURE

1. Where, Where . . . from, What, Who

Where is Amrita?	She's at the store.
Where is Delhi?	It's in India.
Where is François from?	He's from Haiti.
Where are Kenji and Hiroko from?	They're from Japan.
What is in the drawer?	Pens, papers, and files are in the drawer.
What is that?	It's a new computer.
Who is the man next to Amrita?	It's Ram.
Who is Hiroko's husband?	Kenji is Hiroko's husband.

2. I don't have any . . .

Ram doesn't have a stamp.	Ram doesn't have <u>any</u> stamp<u>s</u>.
You don't have the new book.	You don't have <u>any</u> new book<u>s</u>.

We don't have a pen.	We don't have <u>any</u> pen<u>s</u>.
Mrs. Ramirez doesn't have a son.	She doesn't have <u>any</u> son<u>s</u>.
I don't have the file.	I don't have <u>any</u> file<u>s</u>.

3. Do you have any . . . ?

Do you have a stamp?	Do you have <u>any</u> stamp<u>s</u>?
Does she have a pen?	Does she have <u>any</u> pen<u>s</u>?
Do they have the newspaper?	Do they have <u>any</u> newspaper<u>s</u>?
Does he have a brother?	Does he have <u>any</u> brother<u>s</u>?

4. Tuesday / on Tuesday / Tuesdays

Today is Tuesday.	The bank is open <u>on Tuesday</u>.
	The bank is open <u>Tuesdays</u>.
Today is Saturday.	Maria is not in the office <u>on Saturday</u>.
	Maria is not in the office <u>Saturdays</u>.

Today is Wednesday.	The store is closed <u>on Wednesday</u>.
	The store is closed <u>Wednesdays</u>.
Today is Sunday.	The post office is closed <u>on Sunday</u>.
	The post office is closed <u>Sundays</u>.

5. in, from, at, on

in	San Francisco is in the USA.
	The Statue of Liberty is in New York.
from	Hiroko and Kenji are from Japan.
	John is not from Boston. He's from New York.
at	Maria is at the office, Ram is at the post office, and Amrita is at the store.
	There are very good books at the library.
on	The books are on the bookshelf.
	The police station is on Second Street, and the school is on Hill Avenue.

EXERCISES

A. Natasha doesn't have a book.
Natasha doesn't have any books.

1. Ram doesn't have a daughter.

   _____.

2. John doesn't have a stamp.

   _____.

3. We don't have the file.

   _____.

4. Hiroko doesn't have a dog.

   _____.

5. He doesn't have a good magazine.

   _____.

6. She doesn't have a cousin.

   _____.

B. Do you have a brother?
Do you have any brothers?

1. Do you have a sister?

   _____.

2. Does Amrita have a daughter?

_____.

3. Do they have a Russian book?

_____.

4. Do we have a black pen?

_____.

5. Does he have a cousin in New York?

_____.

6. Do they have a good CD?

_____.

C. The bank is not open ___(Sunday)___.
The bank is not open Sundays.
The bank is not open on Sunday.

1. The children are in school ___(Monday)___.

_____.

_____.

2. The post office is open ___(Thursday)___.

_____.

_____.

3. Mrs. Sandoval is at the office ____(Friday)____.

   _____.

   _____.

4. The library is open ____(Saturday)____.

   _____.

   _____.

5. The store is closed ____(Sunday)____.

   _____.

   _____.

D. 1. Mr. and Mrs. Sandoval are (on/at)
   _____ the hotel.

2. The shoe store is (on/in) _____
   Third Street.

3. Akira is (on/in) _____ the living
   room.

4. Natasha is (from/on) _____ Russia.

5. The Statue of Liberty is not (on/in)
   _____ Miami.

6. The children are (at/from) _____
   school.

7. Are you (at/on) _____ the supermarket?

8. Los Angeles, San Diego, and San Francisco are (at/in) _____ California.

A. 1.Ram doesn't have any daughters. 2. John doesn't have any stamps. 3. We don't have any files. 4. Hiroko doesn't have any dogs. 5. He doesn't have any good magazines. 6. She doesn't have any cousins.

B. 1. Do you have any sisters? 2. Does Amrita have any daughters? 3. Do they have any Russian books? 4. Do we have any black pens? 5. Does he have any cousins in New York? 6. Do they have any good CDs?

C. 1. Mondays, on Monday, 2. Thursdays, on Thursday, 3. Fridays, on Friday, 4. Saturdays, on Saturday, 5. Sundays, on Sunday

D. 1. at, 2. on, 3. in, 4. from, 5. in, 6. at, 7. at, 8. in

WORD STUDY

go to New York

go

read a book

write a letter

use the computer

go on the Internet

They're at the library.

Natasha is here, and Ram is there.

walk

| This is a black dog. | This is a black dog, too. | Every dog is black. | All the dogs are black. |

DIALOGUE

Natasha: **Amrita, is the library open on Saturday?**

Amrita: **Yes, it is. I go to the library every Saturday.**

Natasha: **What do you do there?**

Amrita: **I read there, and I write letters there, too.**

Natasha: **Are there any computers at the library?**

Amrita: **Yes, there are. I use the computers at the library. All the computers at the library are new.**

Natasha: **What do you do there?**

Amrita: **I go on the Internet. I write e-mail to my sister in Mumbai.**

Natasha: **Does Ram go to the library, too?**

Amrita: **No, he doesn't.**

Natasha: **What does he do?**

Amrita: **Ram walks in the park on Saturday.**

VOCABULARY

go	library
to	at
read a book	walk
write a letter	here
use the computer	there
go on the Internet	every
walk	write
run	speak
sit	sing
stand	watch television
eat	listen to music
drink	use the computer
sleep	jog
swim	drive
play basketball	
ride a bike	
read	

STRUCTURE

1. read / reads

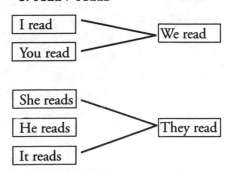

I read the newspaper every Sunday.

You read magazines every day.

John and Sarah write letters.

Hiroko, Kenji, Chikako, and Akira eat in the dining room.

We sleep in the bedroom.

He reads in the office.

Maria uses the computer in the office.

Ram writes at the library.

The dog runs in the park.

2. I read . . . / Do I read . . . ?

I read good books.	Do I read good books?
You go to the library every Saturday.	Do you go to the library every Saturday?
We listen to music.	Do we listen to music?
They watch TV in the living room.	Do they watch TV in the living room?
She writes letters.	Does she write letters?
He runs in the park.	Does he run in the park?

3. don't read / doesn't read

I read good books.	I don't read good books.
You go to the library every Saturday.	You don't go to the library every Saturday.
We listen to music.	We don't listen to music.
They watch TV in the living room.	They don't watch TV in the living room.
She writes letters.	She doesn't write letters.

He runs in the park.   He doesn't run in the park.

4. Yes, I do. / No, I don't.

Do I read good books?	Yes, I do.	No, I don't.
Do you go to the library every Saturday?	Yes, you do.	No, you don't.
Do we listen to music?	Yes, we do.	No, we don't.
Do they watch TV in the living room?	Yes, they do.	No, they don't.
Does she write letters?	Yes, she does.	No, she doesn't.
Does he run in the park?	Yes, he does.	No, he doesn't.

5. There isn't a . . . / There aren't any . . .

There is a cup on the table.

There isn't a cup on the table.

There aren't any cups on the table.

There is a good restaurant here.

There isn't a good restaurant here.

There aren't any good restaurants here.

6. Is there a . . . ? / Are there any . . . ?

Is there a book on the table?

Are there <u>any</u> book<u>s</u> on the table?

Is there a library here?

Are there <u>any</u> librarie<u>s</u> here?

Is there a CD in the living room?

Are there <u>any</u> CD<u>s</u> in the living room?

Is there an old file at the office?

Are there <u>any</u> old file<u>s</u> at the office?

EXERCISES

A. 1. The children (walk/walks) _____ to school.

2. The dog (run/runs) _____ from the house.

3. Ram (sit/sits)_____ and (read/reads)_____ the newspaper.

4. They (stand/stands) _____ and (speak/speaks)_____.

5. John (watch/watches) _____ television in the living room.

6. She (sing/sings) _____ at church every Sunday.

7. He (use/uses) _____ the computer at the library.

8. They (drive/drives) _____ to the office, and you (walk/walks) _____.

9. I (listen/listens) _____ to music in my bedroom.

10. We (swim/swims) _____ at the park.

B. 1. (Do/Does) _____ she go to school on Saturday?

2. (Do/Does) _____ they use the computer at the office?

3. (Do/Does) _____ you speak Russian?

4. (Do/Does) _____ he drive or walk to the office?

5. (Do/Does) _____ we have any stamps?

6. (Do/Does) _____ they read at school?
7. (Do/Does) _____ I have your book?
8. (Do/Does) _____ he jog in the park?

C. I read in my bedroom.
I don't read in my bedroom.

1. You speak Japanese.

_____.

2. We eat in the dining room.

_____.

3. She sleeps on the couch.

_____.

4. Maria uses the computer at the office.

_____.

5. Ram goes to the post office.

_____.

6. We write letters.

_____.

D. He reads at the library.
Does he read at the library?

1. She sleeps in a big bed.

   _____.

2. He uses a new computer at work.

   _____.

3. We read at the library.

   _____.

4. You speak English.

   _____.

5. Natasha speaks Russian.

   _____.

6. They jog in the park.

   _____.

E. Is there a magazine in the living room?
Are there any magazines in the living room?

1. Is there a file in the drawer?

   _____.

2. Is there a picture on the wall?

   _____.

3. Is there an Indian restaurant here?

   _____.

4. Is there a shoe store in the town?

   _____.

5. Is there a stamp on the letter?

   _____.

6. Is there a Russian book at the library?

   _____.

A. 1.walk, 2. runs, 3. sits, reads, 4. stand, speak, 5. watches, 6. sings, 7. uses, 8. drive, walk, 9. listen, 10. swim

B. 1. Does, 2. Do, 3. Do, 4. Does, 5. Do, 6. Do, 7. Do, 8. Does

C. 1. You don't speak Japanese. 2. We don't eat in the dining room. 3. She doesn't sleep on the couch. 4. Maria doesn't use the computer at the office. 5. Ram doesn't go to the post office. 6. We don't write letters.

D. 1. Does she sleep in a big bed? 2. Does he use a new computer at work? 3. Do we read at the library? 4. Do you speak English? 5. Does Natasha speak Russian? 6. Do they jog in the park?

E. 1. Are there any files in the drawer? 2. Are there any pictures on the wall? 3. Are there any Indian restaurants here? 4. Are there any shoe stores in town? 5. Are there any stamps on the letter? 6. Are there any Russian books at the library?

Let's Go to the Beach Today!

WORD STUDY

Today is Monday, but John doesn't work today.
He <u>has the day off</u>.

Do you have today off?
Yes, I do.

This is the sun.
It's a sunny day.

This is the beach.
People swim at the
beach.

It's cold!   It's cool.   It's warm.   It's hot!

This bus is crowded. There are too many people on it.

 not finished

still not finished

 not finished yet

almost finished

finished!

The children <u>talk</u>.

The girl <u>talks</u> to the boy.

She <u>tells</u> him <u>about</u> the beach.

She <u>says</u>, "The beach is beautiful!"

He <u>hears</u> "The beach is beautiful!"

The boy <u>understands</u> the girl.

The boy doesn't <u>understand</u> the girl.

He doesn't understand <u>because</u> he doesn't speak Spanish.

He says, "I don't understand."

DIALOGUE

Maria: Hello?

Natasha: Hi, Maria, it's Natasha.

Maria: Hi, Natasha.

Natasha: Maria, do you work today?

Maria: No, I have the day off.

Natasha: It's a beautiful, sunny day.

Maria: It is. Hey, let's go to the beach today!

Natasha: Yes! That's a great idea. I like the beach. I hear that the water is warm.

Maria: My coworkers tell me that the beach isn't very crowded, too.

Natasha: I understand that. It's not summer yet, so the water is still too cold for swimming.

Maria: Well, let's lie in the sun.

Natasha: Fantastic!

VOCABULARY

umbrella	wave
sunglasses	ocean
sand	bathing suit

The woman stands in the sun.

This woman smiles.

This woman laughs.

The baby cries.

The mother holds the baby.

This boy throws the Frisbee.

The boy catches the Frisbee.

The little girl closes the car door.

Her father opens the trunk of the car.

have the day off	**too many**
sun	**still**
sunny	**not yet**
beach	**almost**
ocean	**talk**
cold	**tell**
cool	**about**
warm	**say**
hot	**hear**
crowded	**understand**

STRUCTURE

1. that

The girl says, "The beach is beautiful!"

She says <u>that</u> the beach is beautiful.

The boy hears, "The beach is beautiful!"

He hears <u>that</u> the beach is beautiful.

Ram tells Amrita, "I have the day off."
He tells her <u>that</u> he has the day off.

Hiroko says, "I'm from Japan."
She says <u>that</u> she's from Japan.

People say, "New York is interesting."
They say <u>that</u> New York is interesting.

Amrita writes, "I'm happy."
Amrita writes <u>that</u> she's happy.

2. Why . . . ? Because . . .

Does this boy understand this girl?
No, he doesn't understand her.

<u>Why</u> doesn't he understand her?
He doesn't understand her <u>because</u> she speaks Spanish.

<u>Why</u> does Ram have the day off?
<u>Because</u> it's Sunday.

<u>Why</u> isn't the beach crowded?
<u>Because</u> it isn't summer yet.

<u>Why</u> don't the people swim?
<u>Because</u> the water is still too cold.

3a. too (1)

Ram is from India.

Amrita is from India, too.

He has a small apartment.

She has a small apartment, too.

3b. too (2)

This car is wide.

This street is very
narrow.

This car is <u>too</u> wide.

This street is <u>too</u>
narrow.

They say that New York is <u>too</u> big.

Alaska is <u>too</u> cold, but Florida is <u>too</u> hot.

4. for

Amrita: Natasha, here,
   this gift is *for* you.
Natasha: A gift *for* me?
   Thanks, Amrita.
Amrita: Happy birthday!

This new keyboard is <u>for</u> my computer.

The letter is <u>for</u> Amrita's sister.

It's too cold today <u>for</u> swimming.

Alaska is too cold <u>for</u> me!

New York is too big <u>for</u> my sister, and her town is too small <u>for</u> me.

EXERCISES

A. The girl says, "The beach is beautiful."
   The girl says that the beach is beautiful.

   1. John says, "The day is sunny."

   _____.

2. Amrita says, "All the computers at the library are new."

_____.

3. People say, "New York is too big."

_____.

4. François says, "The bank is closed today."

_____.

5. Maria tells Natasha, "I'm going to the office."

_____.

6. John tells Ram, "I have a new car."

_____.

B. Why doesn't the boy understand the girl? (He doesn't speak Spanish.)

The boy doesn't understand the girl because he doesn't speak Spanish.

1. Why aren't the children at school? (It's Saturday.)

_____.

2. Why doesn't the girl swim? (The water is too cold.)

   _____.

3. Why doesn't John smile? (He isn't happy.)

   _____.

4. Why do they have sunglasses? (It's very sunny.)

   _____.

C. 1. The baby _____. (holds/cries)

2. They lie _____ (above/under) the umbrella.

3. John has the day _____ (on/off) today.

4. It's not summer _____ (yet/still), so the water is cold.

5. The dog _____ (catches/understands) the Frisbee.

6. The girl's father _____ (holds/closes) the trunk of the car.

A. 1. *John says that the day is sunny.* 2. *Amrita says that all the computers at the library are new.* 3. *People say that New York is too big.* 4. *François says that the bank is closed today.* 5. *Maria tells Natasha that she's going to the office.* 6. *John tells Ram that he has a new car.*

B. 1. *The children aren't at school because it's Saturday.* 2. *The girls doesn't swim because the water is too cold.* 3. *John doesn't smile because he isn't happy.* 4. *They have sunglasses because it's very sunny.*

C. 1. *cries,* 2. *under,* 3. *off,* 4. *yet,* 5. *catches,* 6. *closes*

...tired.

He eats a lot.

go to bed

6:00 (six o'clock)

morning

noon

afternoon

evening

night

Maria gets to the office at 8:00.

Maria leaves work at 6:00.

She wakes up early, and he wakes up late.

❧ DIALOGUE

 Maria: **I'm tired today.**

Hiroko: **Well, you work a lot.**

John: **Where do you work, Maria?**

Maria: **I work in an office. I wake up very early every day.**

Hiroko: **And she works very late, too.**

John: **What time do you wake up?**

Maria: **I wake up at 6:00 in the morning, and I get to work at 8:00.**

John: **That's very early! And when do you leave work?**

Maria: **I leave work at 6:30 or 7:00 in the evening.**

John: **7 o'clock? That's late.**

Hiroko: **You work too much!**

VOCABULARY

tired	afternoon
a little	evening
a lot	night
too much	work
wake up	gets to
go to bed	leaves
6:00 (six o'clock)	wakes up
morning	early
noon	late

morning   noon

afternoon   evening

night

We eat breakfast in the morning.

We eat lunch at noon.

We eat dinner in the evening.

We sleep at night.

20	twenty	31	thirty-one
21	twenty-one	32	thirty-two
22	twenty-two	33	thirty-three
23	twenty-three	40	forty
24	twenty-four	50	fifty
25	twenty-five	60	sixty
26	twenty-six	70	seventy
27	twenty-seven	80	eighty
28	twenty-eight	90	ninety
29	twenty-nine	100	one hundred
30	thirty		

AN HOUR

There are 60 minutes in an hour.

There are 60 seconds in a minute.

There are 24 hours in a day.

There are 7 days in a week.

STRUCTURE

1. 1:00, 2:00 . . .

What time is it?

It's one o'clock.   It's two o'clock.

It's six o'clock.   It's five-thirty.

It's nine-thirty.

It's eight forty-five.

It's eleven-fifteen.

It's two fifty-three.

It's noon.

It's midnight.

2. at 1:00, at 2:00 . . .

Maria gets to work at 8:00.

Maria leaves work at 6:30.

The children get to school at 7:30 in the morning.

They leave school at 3:00 in the afternoon.

3. (At) what time . . . ? / When . . . ?

At what time does Ram get to the library?
He gets to the library at 1:30.

When does Ram get to the library?
He gets to the library at 1:30.

What time do the children go to school?
They go to school at 7:00 A.M.

When do they get to school?
They get to school at 7:20.

4. A.M. / P.M.

It's three o'clock in the morning
= It's three o'clock A.M.

It's nine o'clock in the morning
= It's nine o'clock A.M.

It's eleven o'clock in the morning
= It's eleven o'clock A.M.

It's one o'clock in the afternoon
= It's one o'clock P.M.

It's six o'clock in the evening
= It's six o'clock P.M.

It's ten o'clock in the evening
= It's ten o'clock P.M.

5. Morning, noon, afternoon, evening, night

I wake up at 6:30 <u>in the morning</u>.

I eat breakfast at 7:30 <u>in the morning</u>.

I eat lunch <u>at noon</u>.

I go to the bank at 3:00 <u>in the afternoon</u>.

I leave work at 6:00 <u>in the evening</u>.

I eat dinner at 6:30 <u>in the evening</u>.

I go to bed at 11:30 <u>at night</u>.

6. a house / an hour

<u>A</u>   +   b, c, d, f, g, j, k, l, m, n, p, qu, r, s, t, v, w, x, y, z

<u>AN</u> +   a, e, i, o, u,

<u>A/AN</u> +   h

Amrita works at <u>a</u> bookstore.

Maria works in <u>an</u> office.

There are 60 minutes in <u>an</u> hour.

There is <u>a</u> hotel next to the train station.

Dr. Patel works in <u>a</u> hospital.

EXERCISES

A. 7:00

It's seven o'clock.

1. 1:00

_____.

2. 5:30

_____.

3. 7:45

_____.

4. 11:00

_____.

5. 3:30

_____.

6. 2:15

_____.

7. 9:37

_____.

8. 12:45

_____.

B. At what time does Maria wake up? (6:00 in the morning)
She wakes up at 6:00 in the morning.

1. At what time does Maria get to the office? (8:00 in the morning)

_____.

2. When does Ram leave the library? (4:30 in the afternoon)

   _____.

3. When does Chikako wake up on Saturday? (10:00 A.M.)

   _____.

4. What time does Natasha eat lunch? (12:30 in the afternoon)

   _____.

5. When is the bank closed? (Sundays)

   _____.

6. What time do Ram and Amrita eat dinner? (6:00 in the evening)

   _____.

7. When do Hiroko and Kenji watch television? (8:00 in the evening)

   _____.

8. When do the children go to bed? (11:00 at night)

   _____.

C. 1. John wakes up at 7:30 in (the/a/an)

_____ morning.

2. There are sixty minutes in (the/a/an)

_____ hour.

3. There are seven days in (the/a/an)

_____ week.

4. We eat lunch at 1:00 in (the/a/an)

_____ afternoon.

5. They have (the/a/an) _____ old car.

6. The doctor works in (the/a/an)

_____ hospital.

A. 1. *It's one o'clock. 2. It's five-thirty. 3. It's seven forty-five. 4. It's eleven o'clock. 5. It's three-thirty. 6. It's two-fifteen. 7. It's nine thirty-seven. 8. It's twelve forty-five.*

B. 1. *She gets to the office at 8:00 in the morning. 2. He leaves the library at 4:30 in the afternoon. 3. She wakes up at 10:00 A.M. on Saturday. 4. She eats lunch at 12:30 in the afternoon. 5. It's closed Sundays. 6. They eat dinner at 6:00 in the evening. 7. They watch television at 8:00 in the evening. 8. They go to bed at 11:00 at night.*

C. 1. *the, 2. an, 3. a, 4. the, 5. an, 6. the*

Where's the Cereal?

This is cereal.

This is juice.

bowl

bottle

box

can

carton

bag

glass

jar

package

This is a supermarket.
This is an aisle in a supermarket.

Ram has milk.   François is <u>out of</u> milk.

There's milk <u>left</u>.   There's <u>no</u> milk <u>left</u>.

                         François <u>needs</u> milk.

This is an apple.   This is an orange.

There are <u>some</u> apples, <u>some</u> oranges, <u>some</u> juice, <u>some</u> milk, and <u>some</u> cereal on the table.

 DIALOGUE

François: **Excuse me, where's the cereal?**
Clerk: **The cereal's in aisle three.**
François: **Thank you.**
Clerk: **No problem.**
Alison: **Do we have any milk?**
François: **No, we don't. We're out of milk. We**

need two boxes of cereal, a carton of milk,
some bread, a bag of sugar, and a carton
of eggs.

Alison: **And a bottle of juice. We're out of
juice.**

François: **Apple juice or orange juice?**

Alison: **Orange juice. I don't like apple juice.**

François: **Okay. Orange juice.**

VOCABULARY

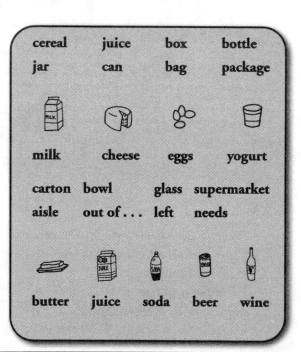

| meat | | chicken | | beef |
| pork | | steak | | turkey |

| sausage | bacon | apples | oranges |

| grapes | bananas | cherries | coffee | tea |

| sugar | potatoes | lettuce | tomatoes |

| cucumbers | mushrooms | carrots | celery |
| spinach | beans |

a loaf of bread   cake   cookies

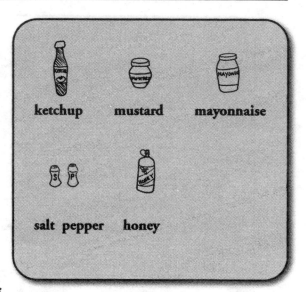

ketchup   mustard   mayonnaise

salt pepper   honey

STRUCTURE

1. one box, two box**es**

-x, -ch, -sh -ss → -xes, -ches, -shes, -sses

one box	two boxes
a fax	faxes
one church	some churches
a glass	two glasses

-f, -fe → -ves

bookshelf	bookshelves

wife	wives
loaf	loaves

-y → -ies

a library	two libraries
a cherry	some cherries
the man	the men
woman	women
child	some children
man, woman, child	people

2. some

There are some apples on the table.

There are some oranges on the table.

There is some juice in the bottle.

There is some milk in the glass.

There is some cereal in the bowl.

3. of

This is a box of cereal.   This is a bottle of
                            juice.

Ram has a map <u>of</u> India.

John drinks a glass <u>of</u> orange juice every
morning.

We need a carton <u>of</u> milk.

There is a picture <u>of</u> the Statue of Liberty on
the wall.

 EXERCISES

A. bread
   There's no bread left.
   We're out of bread.

   1. juice

   _____.

   _____.

   2. tomatoes

   _____.

   _____.

3. sugar

   _____.

   _____.

4. oranges

   _____.

   _____.

5. coffee

   _____.

   _____.

B. There is <u>a book</u> on the bookshelf.
   There are books on the bookshelf.

1. Natasha has <u>the box</u> of cereal.

   _____.

2. <u>The church</u> is next to the park.

   _____.

3. <u>The hotel</u> is next to the train station.

   _____.

4. <u>The loaf</u> of bread is in aisle two.

   _____.

5. <u>The child</u> plays next to the school.

   _____.

6. <u>The cherry</u> is under the table.

   _____.

7. <u>The woman</u> in the car is Russian.

   _____.

8. John speaks to <u>the man</u> on the sidewalk.

   _____.

C. There is <u>a banana</u> in the bowl.
   There are some bananas in the bowl.

1. Ram eats <u>an orange</u> every morning.

   _____.

2. I have <u>a pen</u> in the drawer.

   _____.

3. The boys eats <u>a cookie</u>.

   _____.

4. There is <u>a carrot</u> in the bag.

   _____.

5. <u>A boy</u> and <u>a girl</u> are at school.

   _____.

6. We need <u>an egg</u>.

_____.

D. 1. John has a picture (of/from) _____
New York on the wall.

2. The bread is (at/in) _____ aisle two.

3. We go (in/to) _____ the
supermarket every Saturday.

4. There is a bowl (in/of) _____
cherries (on/in) _____ the table.

5. The supermarket is (at/next to)
_____ the shoe store.

6. Maria gets (to/at) _____ the office
early in the morning.

7. The bus goes (in/to) _____ Boston
every afternoon.

8. Do you have a map (of/from)
_____ the USA?

A. 1. There's no juice left. We're out of juice.
2. There are no tomatoes left. We're out of toma-
toes. 3. There's no sugar left. We're out of sugar.
4. There are no oranges left. We're out of oranges.
5. There's no coffee left. We're out of coffee.

B. 1. *Natasha has the boxes of cereal.* 2. *The churches are next to the park.* 3. *The hotels are next to the train station.* 4. *The loaves of bread are in aisle two.* 5. *The children play next to the school.* 6. *The cherries are under the table.* 7. *The women in the car are Russian.* 8. *John speaks to the men on the sidewalk.*

C. 1. *Ram eats some oranges every morning.* 2. *I have some pens in the drawer.* 3. *The boys eat some cookies.* 4. *There are some carrots in the bag.* 5. *Some boys and some girls are at school.* 6. *We need some eggs.*

D. 1. *of,* 2. *in,* 3. *to,* 4. *of, on,* 5. *next to,* 6. *to,* 7. *to,* 8. *of*

How Much Does This Shirt Cost?

The dog is <u>black</u>.

The <u>shirt</u> is <u>white</u>.

Apples are <u>red</u>.

Bananas are <u>yellow</u>.

Oranges are <u>orange</u>.

Grapes are <u>purple</u>.

The ocean is <u>blue</u>.

Elephants are <u>gray</u>.

The big leaf is <u>green</u>.

The little leaf is <u>brown</u>.

Black, white, red, yellow, orange, purple, blue, gray, green, brown, and orange are <u>colors.</u>

The white shirt is a <u>size small</u>, and it <u>costs</u> $20.00.

The black shirt is a <u>size medium</u>, and it <u>costs</u> $20.00, too.

The black and white shirt is a <u>size large</u>, and it is <u>on sale for $25.00.</u>

The <u>price</u> of the black and white shirt is $5.00. It's <u>cheap</u>.

The <u>price</u> of the white shirt is $95.00. It's <u>expensive</u>.

cash   check   credit card

Natasha <u>buys</u> a
shirt.
The saleswoman
<u>sells</u> the shirt.

Natasha <u>pays</u> for
the shirt.
She <u>pays</u> cash.

Natasha <u>gives</u> the cash to the saleswoman.
The saleswoman <u>takes</u> the cash.

 DIALOGUE

Maria: **Hiroko, look at this blue shirt!**
Hiroko: **It's beautiful. Is it your size?**
Maria: **Yes, it is. It's a medium. But I don't see the price.**
Hiroko: **Ask the salesperson.**
Maria: **Excuse me, how much does this shirt cost?**
Salesperson: **That shirt costs $25.00, but it's on sale for $15.00. Do you like it?**

Maria: **Yes, I do.**

Hiroko: **It's not very expensive. A good price for that shirt is $15.00.**

Maria: **Do you take credit cards?**

Salesperson: **Of course. We take cash, checks, or credit cards.**

VOCABULARY

black	medium
white	large
red	cost
yellow	on sale
orange	price
purple	cheap
blue	expensive
gray	buy
green	sell
brown	pay
colors	give
size	take
small	

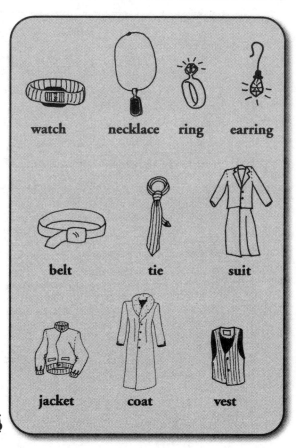

watch   necklace   ring   earring

belt   tie   suit

jacket   coat   vest

STRUCTURE

1. this, that, these, those

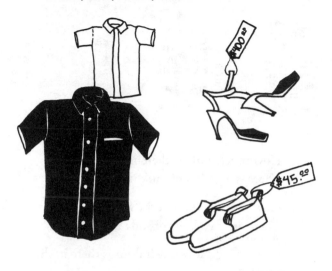

This shirt is black, and that shirt is white.

These shoes are cheap, and those shoes are expensive.

This computer is new, but that computer is old.

These pants are on sale, but those pants are not on sale.

2. How much?

How much milk is there in the carton?
There is a gallon of milk in the carton.

How much soda is in the bottle?
There are two liters of soda in the bottle.

How much flour is there in the bag?
There are five pounds of flour in the bag.

How much beer is there in the bottle?
There are twelve ounces of beer in the bottle.

3. How many?

How many bananas are there in this picture?
There are three bananas in this picture.

How many socks are there in this picture?
There are two socks in this picture.

How many cups are there in this picture?
There are five cups in this picture.

How many rings are there in this picture?
There are four rings in this picture.

How many apples are there in this picture?
There is one apple in this picture.

4. a lot of, a little, a few, too much, too many

How much?   a lot of . . .   a little . . .

How many?   a lot of . . .   a few . . .

There's a lot of water in the ocean.

There's a little water in my glass.

There's too much work for me today!

There are too many books on that shelf!

There are a lot of people on the street in the afternoon.

There are a few people on the street at night.

There are too many people in this room!

5. (please) ask, (please) look, (please) take . . .

Hiroko says, "Come in, Ram! Please, sit down!"

Ask the saleswoman the price of this shirt.

Look at this beautiful blouse!

Please take this book and read it.

Go to the store and buy a gallon of milk.

6. (please) don't smoke, (please) don't run, (please) don't speak . . .

The teacher says, "Children, don't run!"

The waiter says, "Please don't smoke in the restaurant."

Don't pay too much for that shirt.

Don't go to the beach this weekend. It's too cold!

Don't speak in the library.

 EXERCISES

A. shirt

How much does that shirt cost?

gloves

How much do those gloves cost?

1. pants

   _____.

2. hat

   _____.

3. belt

   _____.

4. boots

   _____.

5. jacket

   _____.

6. jeans

   _____.

B. 1. _____ shirt is black.

2. _____ shirt is white.

3. _____ shoes are cheap.

4. _____ shoes are expensive.

5. (This/These) _____ people work in my office.

6. (This/These) _____ pants are not very expensive.

7. (That/Those) _____ magazine is not very good.

8. There is a lot of juice in (that/those) _____ glasses.

9. Take (this/these) _____ CD and
   listen to it.

10. Write (this/these) _____ number,
    please.

C. 1. (How much/How many) _____
   coffee is in this cup?

2. (How much/How many) _____
   sugar do you take in your tea?

3. (How much/How many) _____
   shirts in this store are on sale?

4. (How much/How many) _____
   milk is left?

5. (How much/How many) _____
   CDs do you have?

6. (How much/How many) _____
   people are in this town?

7. (How much/How many) _____
   brothers does John have?

8. (How much/How many) _____
   water is there in the ocean?

D. 1. I have (a little/a few) _____ dollars.

2. I take (a little/a few) _____ sugar in
   my coffee.

3. François has (a little/a few) _____ brown suits.

4. There is (a little/a few) _____ salt left.

5. Maria has (a little/a few) _____ credit cards.

6. Mrs. Ramirez has (a little/a few) _____ wine left in the glass.

7. There are (a little/a few) _____ files in the drawer.

8. Go to the store and buy (a little/a few) _____ bottles of soda.

A. 1. *How much do those pants cost?* 2. *How much does that hat cost?* 3. *How much does that belt cost?* 4. *How much do those boots cost?* 5. *How much does that jacket cost?* 6. *How much do those jeans cost?*

B. 1. *This,* 2. *That,* 3. *These,* 4. *Those,* 5. *These,* 6. *These,* 7. *That,* 8. *Those,* 9. *this,* 10. *this*

C. 1. *How much,* 2. *How much,* 3. *How many,* 4. *How much,* 5. *How many,* 6. *How many,* 7. *How many,* 8. *How much*

D. 1. *a few,* 2. *a little,* 3. *a few,* 4. *a little,* 5. *a few,* 6. *a little,* 7. *a few,* 8. *a few*

What Do You Do?

The <u>question</u> is "What's 8 + 8?" and the <u>answer</u> is "16."

The teacher <u>asks</u> the question.

The students <u>know</u> the answer.

A student <u>answers</u> the question.

The question is <u>easy</u>.

The students <u>don't know</u> the answer.

This question is not easy, it's <u>difficult</u>.

John <u>knows</u> François.
They are <u>friends</u>.

John <u>doesn't know</u> the woman. The woman is a <u>stranger</u>.

They are husband and wife.

They're <u>married</u>.

They're <u>boyfriend and girlfriend</u>.

They're <u>not married</u>.

Hello!

Jose is a policeman.

Ram is a computer technician.

Maria is an office supervisor.

That's <u>exciting</u>!   This book is not <u>interesting</u>, it's <u>boring</u>.

DIALOGUE

Ram: **Maria, do you know my wife, Amrita?**
Maria: **No, I don't know her. It's nice to meet you, Amrita.**
Amrita: **It's nice to meet you, too, Maria.**
Maria: **This is my boyfriend, Jose.**

Ram: It's nice to meet you, Jose. What do you do?

Jose: I'm a policeman.

Amrita: A policeman! That's exciting!

Jose: What do you do?

Ram: I'm a computer technician, and Amrita works in a bookstore.

Jose: Those are interesting jobs.

Maria: I like books.

Amrita: I like them, too. Where do you work, Maria?

Maria: I work in an office. I'm an office supervisor.

VOCABULARY

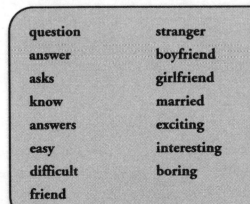

question	stranger
answer	boyfriend
asks	girlfriend
know	married
answers	exciting
easy	interesting
difficult	boring
friend	

Jose is a policeman.

The mail carrier delivers letters.

The taxi driver drives a taxi.

The bus driver drives a bus.

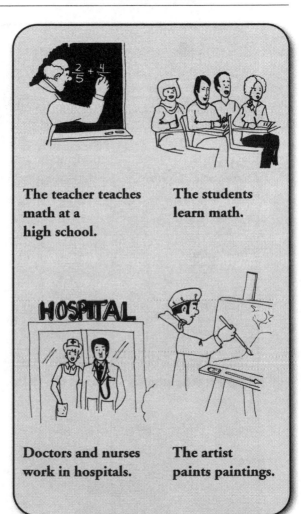

The teacher teaches math at a high school.

The students learn math.

Doctors and nurses work in hospitals.

The artist paints paintings.

Ram is a computer technician.

Maria is an office supervisor.

The receptionist answers the phone.

The security guard watches the video.

The chef cooks.

The waiter works at a restaurant.

The cashier works in a store.

The bank teller takes the money.

Engineers design dams and bridges.

The actor and the actress act in movies.

Singers sing.

The writer writes interesting books.

The mechanic repairs cars.

The painter paints a house.

Construction workers build buildings.

The carpenter makes a table.

The plumber fixes the kitchen sink.

STRUCTURE

1. me, you, him, her, it, us, them

Ram sees John.	Ram sees him.
François sees Natasha.	François sees her.
Natasha sees Hiroko and Kenji.	Natasha sees them.

I	me
you	you
he	him
she	her
it	it
we	us
they	them

Do you know <u>me</u>?

She answers <u>us</u>.

The teacher watches <u>them</u>.

2.this / that; these / those

This is a black shirt, and that is a white shirt.

These are cheap shoes, and those are expensive shoes.

This is John, and that is John's friend.

These are apples, and those are oranges.

3.teach / teaches; watch / watches; fix / fixes

-ch, -x, - sh, -ss + -es

He watches television every evening.

The plumber fixes the kitchen sink.

Mrs. Nelson teaches at the school.

The mother dresses the baby.

EXERCISES

A. Who builds buildings?
Construction workers build buildings.

1. Who designs dams and bridges?

   _____.

2. Who takes the money at the bank?

   _____.

3. Who cooks in a restaurant?

   _____.

4. Who makes tables?

   _____.

5. Who fixes sinks in bathrooms and kitchens?

   _____.

6. Who works in a hospital?

   _____.

7. Who paints paintings?

   _____.

8. Who delivers letters?

   _____.

9. Who drives a taxi?

   _____.

10. Who teaches at universities?

   _____.

B. This is an expensive shirt.
   These are expensive shirts.

That is a black dog.
   Those are black dogs.

1. This is a new disk.

   _____.

2. This is an exciting book.

   _____.

3. That is a stranger.

   _____.

4. This is an easy question.

   _____.

5. That is a good student.

   _____.

C. Ram sees <u>John</u>.
<u>*Ram sees him.*</u>

1. Natasha understands <u>François</u>.

   _____.

2. The policeman talks to <u>Hiroko</u>.

   _____.

3. The little girl watches <u>the doctors and the nurses</u>.

   _____.

4. The students listen to <u>Mrs. Stein.</u>

   _____.

5. Amrita sends <u>her brother</u> a letter.

   _____.

6. Maria stands next to <u>Peter and Janet</u>.

   _____.

A. 1.Engineers design dams and bridges. 2. Bank tellers take money at the bank. 3. Chefs cook at a restaurant. 4. Carpenters make tables. 5. Plumbers fix sinks in bathrooms and kitchens. 6. Doctors and nurses work in hospitals. 7. Artists paint paintings. 8. Mail carriers deliver letters.

9. Taxi drivers drive taxis. 10. Professors teach at universities.

B. 1. These are new disks. 2. These are exciting books. 3. Those are strangers. 4. These are easy questions. 5. Those are good students.

C. 1. Natasha understands him. 2. The policeman talks to her. 3. A little girl watches them. 4. The students listen to her. 5. Amrita sends him a letter. 6. Maria stands next to them.

I'd Like to Make an Appointment.

 WORD STUDY

This is a date book. It's François's date book.

François has an appointment on November sixth at 3:00.

He sees Mrs. Nuñez on that day.

He also has an appointment on Tuesday, November fourth, at 10:00 in the morning.

He's not free at 10:00; he's busy.

  DIALOGUE

Receptionist: **Good morning, Mrs. Nuñez's office.**
François: **Good morning. I'd**

like to make an appointment with Mrs. Nuñez.

Receptionist: Okay, Mrs. Nuñez is free on Tuesday, November fourth, at 10:30 in the morning.

François: Does she have any time in the afternoon?

Receptionist: No, I'm sorry. She's busy in the afternoon on the fourth.

François: How about November sixth?

Receptionist: November sixth at 3:00 is good.

François: That's great.

Receptionist: Your name, please?

François: François Laret.

Receptionist: Could you spell your last name, please?

François: It's L-A-R-E-T.

Receptionist: Okay, Mr. Laret. We'll see you on November sixth at 3:00.

VOCABULARY

appointment	busy
free	see

January	May	September
February	June	October
March	July	November
April	August	December

January is the first month of the year.

February is the second month of the year.

March is the third month of the year.

April is the fourth month of the year.

May is the fifth month of the year.

June is the sixth month of the year.

July is the seventh month of the year.

August is the eighth month of the year.

September is the ninth month of the year.

October is the tenth month of the year.

November is the eleventh month
of the year.

December is the twelfth month
of the year.

January is before February.

March is after February.

winter   spring

summer   fall

In Miami, it's hot in the summer.

In Chicago, it's cold in the winter.

It rains in New York in April.

It snows in Denver in January.

It's sunny and dry in Phoenix, Arizona.

It's wet and cloudy in Seattle.

STRUCTURE

1. would like (I'd like)

I would like to make an appointment with Mrs. Nuñez.

He would like to go to the movies.

I'd like some water, please.

Would you like to see the menu?
Yes, I would. Thank you.

Would you like to speak to Mr. Robinson?
No, I would not.

2. could

Spell your name, please.
Could you spell your name, please?

Give me some water.
Could you give me some water, please?

Excuse me, could I ask you a question?

Could you come in the afternoon?

Could you please tell me where Bank Street is?

EXERCISES

A. Sit down.
Could you please sit down?

1. Take this book.

   _____.

2. Tell me your name.

   _____.

3. Answer the phone.

   _____.

4. Come in the morning.

   _____.

5. Make an appointment.

   _____.

6. Give me those black shoes.

   _____.

B. François makes an appointment.
François would like to make an appointment.

1. Hiroko buys a new blouse.

   _____.

2. Ram goes to the library.

_____.

3. Natasha sees the menu.

_____.

4. Peter speaks Chinese.

_____.

C. 1. This book isn't interesting, it's

_____.

2. The question isn't difficult, it's

_____.

3. Your father isn't fat, he's

_____.

4. Those pants aren't cheap, they're

_____.

5. The street isn't wide, it's

_____.

6. My coffee cup isn't full, it's

_____.

7. The Empire State Building isn't short, it's

_____.

8. Arizona isn't cold, it's

_____.

9. Mrs. Ramirez isn't free today, she's

   _____.

10. I'm not sad, I'm _____.

A. 1. *Could you please take this book? 2. Could you please tell me your name? 3. Could you please answer the phone? 4. Could you please come in the morning? 5. Could you please make an appointment? 6. Could you please give me those black shoes?*

B. 1. *Hiroko would like to buy a new blouse. 2. Ram would like to go to the library. 3. Natasha would like to see the menu. 4. Peter would like to speak Chinese.*

C. 1. *boring,* 2. *easy,* 3. *thin,* 4. *expensive,* 5. *narrow,* 6. *empty,* 7. *tall,* 8. *hot,* 9. *busy,* 10. *happy*

I Don't Feel Good Today!

She <u>feels good</u>.   He doesn't <u>feel good.</u>   She <u>feels dizzy</u>.   He <u>feels nauseous</u>.

John has a <u>headache</u>.
He <u>takes aspirin</u>.

mouth

throat

John has a <u>sore</u> throat.

John's head <u>hurts</u>.

John's throat <u>hurts</u>.

John's <u>stomach</u> <u>hurts</u>.

John is <u>sick</u>. He has <u>the flu</u>.

It's 6:30 <u>now</u>.   It's 3:00 <u>now</u>.   It's 8:45 <u>now</u>.

  DIALOGUE

John: **Dr. Wong, I don't feel good today.
I feel sick.**

Dr. Wong: **Do you have a headache?**

John: **Yes, I have a headache, and I feel dizzy.**

Dr. Wong: **Does your throat hurt?**

John: **Yes, it does. I have a sore throat.**

Dr. Wong: **Open your mouth.**

John: **Ahh . . .**

Dr. Wong: **Your throat's very red. Does your stomach hurt?**

John: **Yes, it does. I feel nauseous.**

Dr. Wong: **Well, I think you have the flu. A lot of people are sick now. You need to stay in bed. Drink a lot of water, and take some aspirin.**

John: **Can I go to work?**

Dr. Wong: **No, you can't. You should stay home and sleep.**

VOCABULARY

feels	hurts
dizzy	think
nauseous	sick
headache	flu
aspirin	now
sore	

THE HUMAN BODY

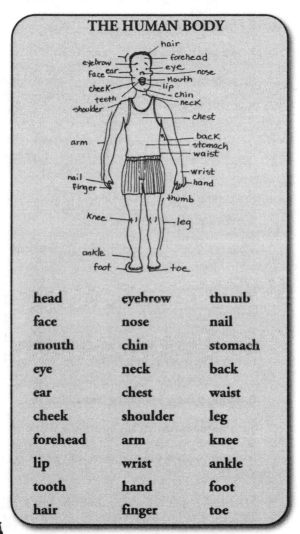

head	eyebrow	thumb
face	nose	nail
mouth	chin	stomach
eye	neck	back
ear	chest	waist
cheek	shoulder	leg
forehead	arm	knee
lip	wrist	ankle
tooth	hand	foot
hair	finger	toe

STRUCTURE

1. my, your, his, her, its, our, their

I am Ram. <u>My</u> name is Ram. <u>My</u> wife is Amrita.

You are Natasha. <u>Your</u> name is Natasha. <u>Your</u> name is Russian.

She is Hiroko. <u>Her</u> name is Hiroko. <u>Her</u> husband is Kenji. <u>Her</u> daughter is Chikako.

He is John. <u>His</u> name is John. <u>His</u> name is American. <u>His</u> apartment is nice.

That is a house. <u>Its</u> door is red. <u>Its</u> walls are white. <u>Its</u> roof is black.

We are Ram and Amrita. <u>Our</u> names are Indian. <u>Our</u> house is big.

They are Hiroko and Kenji. <u>Their</u> children are home. <u>Their</u> car is blue.

2. mine, yours, his, hers, ours, theirs

Your name is American, and <u>mine</u> is Indian.

My computer is old and slow, but <u>yours</u> is new and fast.

Natasha's name is Russian, but not Jose's. <u>His</u> is Spanish.

Jose's sister lives in Venezuela, but not Maria's. <u>Hers</u> lives in the United States.

Their favorite books are in Spanish, but <u>ours</u> are in English.

Our house is small, but <u>theirs</u> is big.

3. need to, have to, want to

This boy is sick. He <u>needs to</u> stay in bed. He <u>needs to</u> rest. He <u>wants to</u> go outside and play.

He <u>needs to</u> stay in bed.
=   He <u>has to</u> stay in bed.

Chikako <u>wants to</u> go to the beach today, but she <u>has to</u> go to school.

She <u>doesn't want to</u> go to school, but she <u>has to</u>.

John <u>wants to</u> stay in bed and sleep, but he <u>has to</u> go to work.

He <u>doesn't want to</u> go to work, but he <u>has to</u>.

Maria and Jose <u>want to</u> watch TV, but it's late and they <u>have to</u> go to bed.

They <u>don't want to</u> work tomorrow, but they <u>have to.</u>

<u>Does</u> Chikako <u>want to</u> go to the beach or to school?
She <u>wants to</u> go to the beach.

<u>Does</u> John <u>want to</u> go to work or stay in bed?
He <u>wants to</u> stay in bed.

What <u>does</u> she <u>have to</u> do?
She <u>has to</u> go to work.

<u>Do</u> Maria and Jose <u>have to</u> go to sleep?
Yes, they do.

4. must, can, should

Chikako and Akira <u>have to</u> go to school.
=   They <u>must</u> go to school.

John <u>has to</u> go to work now.
=   He <u>must</u> go to work now.

I want to buy a new computer, but I only have $100.

I <u>cannot</u> buy a new computer!

I <u>can</u> buy some clothes, but I <u>can't</u> buy a new computer.

Natasha <u>can</u> speak Russian and English, but she <u>can't</u> speak Chinese.

<u>Can</u> you speak Japanese?   No, I <u>can't</u>.

<u>Can</u> they sing?   Yes, they <u>can</u>.

John is sick today.

He <u>should</u> stay home; he <u>shouldn't</u> go to work.

He <u>should</u> sleep; he <u>shouldn't</u> take a walk.

He <u>should</u> take aspirin and drink a lot of water.

 EXERCISES

A. Natasha's name is Russian.

Her name is Russian.

 1. John's apartment is small.

_____ apartment is small.

2. Chikako and Akira's parents are not home.

   _____ parents are not home.

3. I am Mr. Sandoval.

   _____ name is Mr. Sandoval.

4. We have books in English, Spanish, and French.

   _____ books are in English, Spanish, and French.

5. John's car is American, and Maria's car is Japanese.

   _____ car is American, and
   _____ car is Japanese.

B. My friend works in a bookstore, and (your friend) works in an office.

My friend works in a bookstore, and *yours* works in an office.

1. Your apartment is next to the park, and (my apartment) is near the train station.

   _____

   _____

2. Our computer is old, but (their computer) is new.

   _____

   _____

3. His book is interesting, but (her book) is boring.

   _____

   _____

4. My bike is blue, and (his bike) is white.

   _____

   _____

5. Kenji and Chikako's names are Japanese, but (John's and Alison's names) are not.

   _____

   _____

C. 1. It's a beautiful day! I (want to/have to) _____ go to the beach.
2. I don't have a bathing suit. I (want to/need to) _____ buy one.
3. I don't have a car. I (want to/have to) _____ take the bus.

4. The water is cold! I don't (need to/want to) _____ go swimming!

5. It's late. I (have to/want to) _____ go home now.

D. 1. Hiroko _____ speak Japanese. (can, must, should)

2. John is sick and _____ stay in bed. (wants to, can, should)

3. On Saturday they don't _____ go to school. (want to, must, have to)

4. _____ you read Chinese? (should, must, can)

5. Kenji _____ buy a new computer. (needs, need to, needs to)

6. I'm hungry and I _____ eat. (want to, must to, wants to)

7. Does she _____ go to the office now? (needs to, has to, have to)

8. Where does he _____ go? (want to, want, wants to)

A. 1. His; 2. Their; 3. My; 4. Our; 5. His, her

B. 1. Your apartment is next to the park, and mine is near the train station. 2. Our computer is old, but theirs is new. 3. His book is interesting, but hers is boring. 4. My bike is blue, and his is white. 5. Kenji and Chikako's names are Japanese, but theirs are not.

C. 1. want to; 2. need to; 3. have to; 4. want to; 5. have to

D. 1. can; 2. should; 3. have to; 4. Can; 5. needs to; 6. want to; 7. have to, 8. want to

Do You Want to Come with Me?

 WORD STUDY

Natasha <u>speaks</u> Russian and English. Now she <u>is</u> <u>speaking</u> English.

Hi, I'm Natasha.

Ram <u>eats</u> at 6:30. He <u>is not eating</u> now. He<u>'s</u> <u>watching</u> TV.

John <u>teaches</u> English.
He<u>'s not teaching</u>
now. He<u>'s sleeping</u>.

This is an <u>airport</u>.
The <u>passengers</u> are
<u>getting ready</u> to <u>get</u>
<u>on</u> the <u>plane</u>.

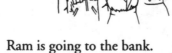

Ram is going to the bank.

<u>Why</u> is he going to the bank?
He's going to the bank <u>to get money</u>.

John is going to the post office.

<u>Why</u> is he going to the post office?
He's going to the post office <u>to get stamps.</u>

John is going to the post office.

He's not <u>coming</u> from the post office. He's <u>coming</u> from his house.

Ram is going to the bank.

He's not <u>coming</u> from the bank. He's <u>coming</u> from the library.

This is Chikako and Akira's grandmother. She's <u>visiting</u> them. She's <u>staying</u> <u>with</u> them at their house.

Is she sitting <u>with</u> <u>anyone</u>?
Yes, she's sitting <u>with</u> Akira and Chikako.

She's not sitting <u>alone</u>.

DIALOGUE

François: Hello, John? This is François.

John: Hi, François. How are you?

François: I'm fine. What are you doing now?

John: I'm getting ready to go to the airport.

François: Why are you going to the airport?

John: I'm going to get my sister. She's coming to stay with me for a few days.

François: You're sister's coming to visit you! That's great! How are you getting to the airport?

John: I'm driving. It's faster than the bus.

François: Is anyone going with you?

John: No, I'm going alone. Do you want to come with me?

François: Sure.

VOCABULARY

speaks	why
airport	come
passengers	visit
plane	stay
get ready	with
get on	alone

Mr. Gordon is
washing the dishes.

He's using detergent
and warm water.

First he puts them
in the water, and
then he takes them
out of the water.

Mrs. Gordon is looking for her car keys.

She has to leave for work, but she can't find her keys.

She always loses them.

Susan is cleaning her bedroom.

She's putting her clothes in the dresser.

Sarah is making her bed.

She's wearing her pajamas.

Jason is taking a shower. He's shaving in the shower.

He's using soap, a razor, and shaving cream.

Every morning he starts to shower at 8:15, and he finishes at 8:30.

He showers for 15 minutes.

Mike is getting dressed. He's putting on his shirt now.

He's looking in a mirror.

STRUCTURE

1. reads / is reading

<u>Ram eats</u> at 6:30 every evening, but <u>he is not eating</u> now.

What <u>is he doing</u> now? <u>He's watching</u> TV now.

EVERY DAY . . .	NOW . . .
I eat.	I am eating. (I'm eating.)
You eat.	You are eating. (You're eating.)
He eats.	He is eating. (He's eating.)
She eats.	She is eating. (She's eating.)
We eat.	We are eating. (We're eating.)
They eat.	They are eating. (They're eating.)

What are you doing now?
I'm reading an interesting book.

Is he sleeping?
No, he's not sleeping. He's taking a shower.

Are they working?
Yes, they are.

Are they buying a new computer?
No, they aren't.

Are you speaking English now?
Yes, I am.

2. Why? to buy stamps, to get milk, etc.

Ram is going to the bank. He's getting money at the bank.

He is going to the bank <u>to get</u> money.

<u>Why</u> is Akira going to the park?
He's going to the park <u>to play</u> with his friends.

<u>Why</u> is Natasha going to the store?
She's going to the store <u>to buy</u> some new clothes.

<u>Why</u> is Amrita driving to the library?
She driving to the library <u>to see</u> Ram.

3. fast, faster, fastest . . . good, better, best . . .

The car is <u>faster.</u>

The dog is <u>fast</u>.

The airplane is <u>the fastest.</u>

-er = more . . .   the -est = the most . . .

California is a big state, but Texas is bigger, and Alaska is the biggest state.

Natasha is a good singer, but Hiroko is better, and Maria is the best singer.

Jim is a bad dancer, but Paul is a worse dancer, and Steve is the worst dancer.

My book is interesting, your book is more interesting, and hers is the most interesting.

Her computer is expensive, yours is more expensive, but mine is the most expensive.

Boston is a big city, but New York is bigger <u>than</u> Boston.

New Jersey is a small state, but Delaware is smaller <u>than</u> New Jersey.

John is tall, but François is taller <u>than</u> John.

4. How?

John is going to the airport.
<u>How</u> is he going?   He's driving.
                                          He's going <u>by car</u>.

Maria is going to the bank.
<u>How</u> is she going?   She's taking the bus.
                                          She's going <u>by bus</u>.

Natasha is going to Chicago.
<u>How</u> is she going?   She's taking the train.
                                          She's going <u>by train</u>.

Kenji is going to Osaka.
<u>How</u> is he going?   He's flying.
                       He's going <u>by plane</u>.

Ram is going to the library.
<u>How</u> is he going?   He's walking.
                       He's going <u>on foot</u>.

5. get

Why is John going to the post office?
He's going to the post office to <u>get</u> stamps.

Where can I get some milk?
You can <u>get</u> milk at the supermarket.

They're going to the airport by bus.
They're <u>getting to</u> the airport by bus.

How is Kenji <u>getting to</u> Osaka?
He's <u>getting to</u> Osaka by plane.

Every morning Chikako <u>gets up</u> at 7:00.

She takes a shower, she <u>gets dressed</u>, and she
eats breakfast.

She <u>gets ready</u> for school.

Chikako takes the bus to school. She <u>gets on</u>

the bus in front of her house, and she
<u>gets off</u> the bus at school. She <u>gets to</u> school
at 8:30.

Maria <u>gets to</u> work by car. She <u>gets in</u> her car at
home, and she <u>gets out of</u> her car in front of
her office. She <u>gets to</u> the office before 9:00
every morning.

You <u>get on</u> a plane, and then you <u>get off</u> the
plane.

You <u>get on</u> a bus, and then you <u>get off</u> the bus.

You <u>get on</u> a train, and then you <u>get off</u> the
train.

You <u>get on</u> a boat, and then you <u>get off</u> the
boat.

You <u>get in</u> a car, and then you <u>get out of</u> the car.

You <u>get in</u> a taxi, and then you <u>get out of</u> the taxi.

You <u>get in</u> bed at night, and you <u>get out of</u> bed in the morning.

EXERCISES

A. John _____ now. (sleep)

John _is sleeping_ now.

1. Natasha _____ Russian with her friends. (speak)
2. That woman _____ in front of the office building. (smoke)
3. You _____ to work now. (go)
4. We _____ on our computers. (work)
5. I _____ some new clothes. (buy)
6. They _____ letters to their friends in Puerto Rico. (write)

B. I'm sleeping.
I'm not sleeping.

1. You're speaking with your friend.

   _____.

2. He's coming to the office now.

   _____.

3. They're eating dinner in the dining room.

   _____.

4. John and François are watching television together.

   _____.

5. The taxi driver is taking our money.

   _____.

6. The plumber is fixing the kitchen sink.

   _____.

7. We're walking in the park.

   _____.

8. I'm listening to the radio.

   _____.

C. They're walking to the post office.
Are they walking to the post office?

1. We're eating in a French restaurant.

   _____.

2. Amrita is speaking Hindi with Ram.

   _____.

3. You're driving to the airport alone.

   _____.

4. They're calling the hospital.

   _____.

D. Why are you going home? (eat dinner)
I'm going home to eat dinner.

1. Why is Maria going to the supermarker?
   (buy milk, eggs, and bread)

   _____.

2. Why are they driving to the beach? (go
   swimming)

   _____.

3. Why are you going to the hospital? (see
   my doctor)

   _____.

4. Why is John getting ready? (go to work)

   _____.

E. Which is faster, a dog or a car? (car)
   A car is faster than a dog.

1. Which is bigger, a house or an apartment
   building? (apartment building)

   _____.

2. Which is smaller, China or Japan? (Japan)

   _____.

3. Who is taller, Hiroko or François?
   (François)

   _____.

4. Who is a better singer, Maria or Natasha?
   (Maria)

   _____.

5. Which city is more interesting, New York
   or Springfield? (New York)

   _____.

6. Which is more expensive, a bike or a car?
   (car)

   _____.

F. 1. I get (on/in) _____ the bus at First Street.

2. Where do you get (out of/off) _____ the train?

3. Natasha is getting (ready/to) _____ for work.

4. We get (at/to) _____ work before 9:00.

5. Get (on/in) _____ the car!

6. What time do you get (up/down) _____ in the morning?

A. 1. is speaking; 2. is smoking; 3. are going; 4. are working; 5. am buying; 6. are writing

B. 1. You're not speaking with your friend. 2. He's not coming to the office now. 3. They're not eating dinner in the dining room. 4. John and François are not watching television together. 5. The taxi driver is not taking our money. 6. The plumber is not fixing the kitchen sink. 7. We're not walking in the park. 8. I'm not listening to the radio.

C. 1. Are we eating in a French restaurant? 2. Is Amrita speaking Hindi with Ram? 3. Are you driving to the airport alone? 4. Are they calling the hospital?

D. 1. Maria is going to the supermarket to buy milk, eggs, and bread. 2. They are driving to the beach to go swimming. 3. I'm going to the hospital to see my doctor. 4. John is getting ready to go to work.

E. 1. An apartment building is bigger than a house. 2. Japan is smaller than China. 3. François is taller than Hiroko. 4. Maria is a better singer than Natasha. 5. New York is a more interesting city than Springfield. 6. A car is more expensive than a bike.

F. 1. on; 2. off; 3. ready; 4. to; 5. in, 6. up

We're Going to Take a Trip This Weekend.

This bag is <u>empty</u>.   This bag is not empty.

There is <u>nothing</u> in it.   There is <u>something</u> in it.

There is <u>nobody</u> in this room.   There is <u>somebody</u> in this room.

There is <u>no one</u> in this room.   There is <u>someone</u> in this room.

This is New York. There are buildings <u>everywhere</u> in New York. John's friend lives <u>somewhere</u> in New York.

This is the country. This is not the city. There are buildings <u>nowhere</u> here. There are <u>mountains</u>, <u>forests</u>, <u>lakes</u>, and <u>rivers</u>. <u>Nobody</u> lives here.

Ram <u>reads</u> every day.

He <u>is reading</u> now.

He's going to <u>read</u> tonight.

He <u>will read</u> tonight.

✵ DIALOGUE

Ram: **Maria, Jose, are you going somewhere?**

Maria: **Yes, we're going to take a trip this weekend. We're going to drive to the country to visit my sister and her family.**

Amrita: **How nice! Where does your sister live?**

Maria: **She lives in a very little town about five hours away.**

Ram: Five hours away? That's far. Will you stop anywhere?

Jose: Sure. We'll stop to eat something.

Maria: And I want to stop at a state park that we'll pass. It's very beautiful. There are mountains and lakes and lots of trees, and nobody is there. I want to take some pictures.

Jose: Maria is someone who's always taking pictures, everywhere we go!

Amrita: Well, have a wonderful trip, and drive carefully!

Maria: Thank you! See you next week!

VOCABULARY

empty	no one
nothing	someone
anything	anywhere
something	everywhere
anybody	somewhere
nobody	nowhere
somebody	

1. mountain	6. lake
2. hill	7. river
3. sky	8. cliff
4. cloud	9. path
5. forest	10. bush

Deer live in the forest.

The deer is jumping over a rock.

The bird is flying over the trees.

The rabbit is hiding under a bush.

> They are camping.
>
> They sleep in a tent.
>
> They cook over a fire.
>
> The girl is smelling a flower.
>
> The man and woman are swimming in the river.
>
> They are having a good time.

 STRUCTURE

1. nothing, something, anything

There's <u>nothing</u> in this bag.	There's <u>something</u> in this bag.
Is there <u>anything</u> in this bag?	Is there <u>anything</u> in this bag?
No, there's <u>nothing</u> in this bag.	Yes, there's <u>something</u> in this bag.

Is there <u>anything to see</u> in San Fransisco?

Yes, there's <u>a lot to see</u> in San Francisco.

Is there <u>anything to eat</u> in the house?

No, there's <u>nothing to eat</u> in the house.

Is there <u>anything good</u> at the movies?

No, there's <u>nothing good</u> at the movies.

Is there <u>anything interesting to do</u> here?

No, there's <u>nothing interesting to do.</u>

2. someone, no one, anyone, somebody, nobody, anybody

There's <u>nobody</u> in this room.

There's <u>somebody</u> in this room.

Is there <u>anybody</u> in this room?

Is there <u>anybody</u> in this room?

| No, there's <u>nobody</u> in this room. | Yes, there's <u>somebody</u> in this room. |

somebody = someone
nobody = no one
anybody = anyone

Is <u>anybody</u> home tonight?	No, <u>nobody</u>'s home tonight.
Is <u>anyone</u> reading this book?	Yes, <u>someone</u> is reading that book.
Is <u>anyone</u> going to the restaurant tonight?	No, <u>nobody</u> is going to the restaurant.

3. somewhere, nowhere, anywhere

Where's my pen? There's a pen <u>somewhere</u> in my bag.

<u>Nowhere</u> in Florida are there mountains.

Are there mountains <u>anywhere</u> in Japan?
Yes, there are.

Are there forests <u>anywhere</u> in New York City?
No, there aren't.

4. everything, everyone, everywhere

<u>Everything</u> in this restaurant is good.

<u>Everyone</u> in Hiroko's family speaks Japanese.

There are taxis <u>everywhere</u> in New York.

5. going to ... / will ...

It's 6:00 now. John isn't eating now, but he's <u>going to eat</u> at 7:00.

We're <u>going to drive</u> to the airport tomorrow.

Are you <u>going to see</u> your family this weekend?

They're <u>going to visit</u> China next year.

You're <u>going to read</u> a book tonight, but <u>you're not going to watch</u> TV.

What <u>am I going to do</u> tomorrow morning?

Next year, I'm going to learn Chinese.
(or)
I <u>will learn</u> Chinese.

Next year, I will learn Chinese.
(or)
I'<u>ll learn</u> Chinese.

Tomorrow, I'<u>ll go</u> to work at 8:00.

You'<u>ll finish</u> that book next week.

When <u>will</u> he <u>come</u> to see us?

What <u>will</u> we <u>buy</u> at the store?

They<u>'ll eat</u> home tonight, but we<u>'ll go</u> to a good restaurant.

6. who . . . / that . . .

Mrs. Yamada is that woman.   She is reading the newspaper.

Mrs. Yamada is that woman <u>who</u> is reading the newspaper.

Mr. Yamada is the man <u>who</u> is sitting next to her.

Natasha is someone <u>who</u> speaks Russian.

Are you someone <u>who</u> watches a lot of TV?

That's someone <u>who</u> works in my office.

I see the car.   John drives the car.

I see the car <u>that</u> John drives.

This is the park <u>that</u> everyone likes.

I'm reading a book <u>that</u> you should read, too.

That's the restaurant <u>that</u> is open twenty-four hours every day.

This is the computer <u>that</u> we'll buy next week.

EXERCISES

A. 1. Is there _____ good on TV tonight?
      (anything/something)

   2. I know _____ who lives in this city.
      (someone/something)

   3. He has _____ good to read on the
      plane. (nobody/something)

   4. Do we have _____ to drink?
      (anything/nothing)

   5. They have _____ to do today.
      (anything/nothing)

   6. My father is _____ in China.
      (somewhere/anywhere)

   7. Are you doing _____ interesting
      this weekend? (nothing/anything)

   8. You should bring _____ to eat on
      the trip. (something/anything)

B. I'm eating a sandwich. (Tomorrow)
   Tomorrow I'm going to eat a sandwich.

   1. We're driving to our friend's house.
      (Tomorrow)

      _____.

2. John is writing a letter to an old friend in London. (After school)

   _____.

3. You're watching something interesting on television. (Tonight)

   _____.

4. We're having dinner at 7:30 tonight. (Tomorrow night)

   _____.

5. The children are learning Spanish. (Next year)

   _____.

6. He's answering my question. (Next week)

   _____.

C. What will she do in Paris? (study French)
   She'll study French in Paris.

   1. What will they eat at the Japanese restaurant? (sushi)

      _____.

2. Who'll drive to the airport tomorrow? (I)

   _____.

3. When will you go to the doctor's?
   (tomorrow afternoon)

   _____.

4. Which shirt will you buy? (the black shirt)

   _____.

5. Who will teach him Russian? (Natasha)

   _____.

6. What will they buy at the department
   store? (a new CD player)

   _____.

D. Mary is the girl. She lives next door.
This is the book. I'm reading it.
Mary is the girl who lives next door.
This is the book that I'm reading.

1. Mrs. Jackson is a woman. She teaches at
   the high school.

   _____.

2. You have a magazine. I want to read it.

   _____.

3. Centerville is a small town. It's not far from here.

_____.

4. On the bus, I sit next to a man. He works with you.

_____.

5. We're visiting a friend. She speaks five languages.

_____.

6. Maria is writing a letter. Her sister will get it next week.

_____.

A. 1. anything; 2. someone; 3. something; 4. anything; 5. nothing; 6. somewhere; 7. anything, 8. something

B. 1. Tomorrow we're going to drive to our friend's house. 2. After school John is going to write a letter to an old friend in London. 3. Tonight you're going to watch something interesting on television. 4. Tomorrow night we're going to have dinner at 7:30. 5. Next year the children are going to learn

Spanish. 6. Next week he's going to answer my question.

C. 1. They'll eat sushi at the Japanese restaurant. 2. I'll drive to the airport tomorrow. 3. I'll go to the doctor's tomorrow afternoon. 4. I'll buy the black shirt. 5. Natasha will teach him Russian. 6. They'll buy a new CD player at the department store.

D. 1. Mrs. Jackson is a woman who teaches at the high school. 2. You have a magazine that I want to read. 3. Centerville is a small town that's not far from here. 4. On the bus, I sit next to a man who works with you. 5. We're visiting a friend who speaks five langauges. 6. Maria is writing a letter that her sister will get next week.

WORD STUDY

Today John <u>is</u> home, but yesterday he <u>was</u> at work.

This year Natasha <u>is</u> in the United States, but last year she <u>was</u> in Russia.

Today is Saturday. Akira and Chikako <u>are</u> home, but yesterday they <u>were</u> at school.

Today Ram is calling Amrita, and yesterday he <u>called</u> her, too.

Today John is going to the bank, and yesterday he <u>went</u> there, too.

Today François and Alison are having dinner at 6:00, and yesterday they <u>had</u> dinner at 6:00, too.

Today, Maria is working, and yesterday she <u>worked</u>, too.

✤ DIALOGUE

Maria: Hi, Amrita!

Amrita: Hello, Maria. Where were you this weekend? I called you, but no one answered the phone.

Maria: Oh, Jose and I were in the country. We went to visit my sister for a few days.

Amrita: How was your trip? Did you have a good time?

Maria: It was great. We had a very good time.

Amrita: Did you and Jose stay with your sister and her family?

Maria: Yes, we did. They have a big house, so we stayed there.

Amrita: What did you do?

Maria: Well, I talked a lot with my sister. We looked at old photos, we walked next to a beautiful river, we drove to a little town and ate dinner in a restaurant.

Amrita: That's great. Welcome back!

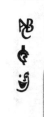

VOCABULARY

am, are, is	was, were
have, has	had
go	went
eat	ate
see	saw
drink	drank
write	wrote
read	read
come	came
sleep	slept
wake	woke
buy	bought
sell	sold
take	took
give	gave
speak	spoke
hear	heard
get	got
run	ran

sit	sat
stand	stood
understand	understood
sing	sang
drive	drove
ride	rode
catch	caught
throw	threw
lie	lay
leave	left
cost	cost
pay	paid
know	knew
teach	taught
hurt	hurt
make	made
do	did
feel	felt
think	thought
find	found
say	said

lose	lost
wear	wore
put	put
tell	told
send	sent
swim	swam
can	could
must	had to

STRUCTURE

1. was, were

Today, I am home.	Yesterday, I <u>was</u> at the hotel.
Today, you're at school.	Yesterday, you <u>were</u> at the doctor's.
He's in his room now.	He <u>was</u> in the living room this morning.
We're in the United States this year.	Last year, we <u>were</u> in Argentina.
They're in their new house this month.	They <u>were</u> in their old house last month.

Where <u>were</u> you last week?	I <u>was</u> in the country last week. .
<u>Was</u> he home last night?	Yes, he <u>was</u>.
<u>Was</u> she at the office yesterday?	No, she <u>wasn't</u> at the office.
Where <u>was</u> she?	She <u>was</u> at the doctor's.
<u>Were</u> they with you last night?	No, they <u>weren't</u> with me.

2. -ed

TODAY	YESTERDAY . . .
Ram talks with Amrita.	He talk<u>ed</u> with her yesterday.
They call their relatives in Mumbai.	They call<u>ed</u> them last week.
The children walk to school.	They walk<u>ed</u> to school.
My cousins play basketball.	My cousins play<u>ed</u> basketball.
He watches TV.	He watch<u>ed</u> TV.

My friend cooks great dinners.	My friend cook<u>ed</u> great dinners.
We listen to the radio.	We listen<u>ed</u> to the radio.
You use the computer.	You us<u>ed</u> the computer.
The plane arrives 2:13.	The plane arriv<u>ed</u> at at 2:13.
She stays late at the office.	She stay<u>ed</u> late at the office.
The mailman delivers a package.	The mailman deliv-er<u>ed</u> a package.
We want to eat early.	We want<u>ed</u> to eat early.

3. go / went; eat / ate

TODAY . . .	YESTERDAY . . .
I have something to do.	I <u>had</u> something to do.
He has a good time.	He <u>had</u> a good time.
They go to school by bus.	They <u>went</u> to school by bus.
We eat dinner at 6:00.	We <u>ate</u> dinner at 6:00.

They see a lot of movies.	They <u>saw</u> a lot of movies.
You drink a glass of water.	You <u>drank</u> a glass of water.
He writes a letter.	He <u>wrote</u> a letter.
She reads an interesting article.	She <u>read</u> an interesting article.
They come to the office by car.	They <u>came</u> to the office by car.
We sleep late.	We <u>slept</u> late.
He wakes up at 7:30.	He <u>woke</u> up at 7:30
Kenji buys a new computer.	Kenji <u>bought</u> a new computer.
The salesman sells me a car.	The salesman <u>sold</u> me a car.
I take sugar in my tea.	I <u>took</u> sugar in my tea.
She gives me a good book to read.	She <u>gave</u> me a good book to read.
We speak Spanish at home.	We <u>spoke</u> Spanish at home.
I hear someone in the hall.	I <u>heard</u> someone in the hall.

You get to the office early.	You <u>got</u> to the office early.
The dog runs in the park.	The dog <u>ran</u> in the park.
I sit next to you.	I <u>sat</u> next to you.
They stand in front of the car.	They <u>stood</u> in front of the car.
I understand him.	I <u>understood</u> him.
Maria sings in Spanish.	Maria <u>sang</u> in Spanish.
Who drives to the supermarket?	Who <u>drove</u> to the supermarket?
I ride my bike to work.	I <u>rode</u> my bike to work.
We leave at 1:30.	We <u>left</u> at 1:30.
The shirt costs $20.	The shirt <u>cost</u> $20.
She pays with a credit card.	She <u>paid</u> with a credit card.
I know that woman.	I <u>knew</u> that woman.
Mrs. Chi teaches math.	Mrs. Chi <u>taught</u> math.
My head hurts!	My head <u>hurt</u>.

The carpenter makes a table.	The carpenter <u>made</u> a table.
I do the dishes.	I <u>did</u> the dishes.
John feels sick.	John <u>felt</u> sick.
He thinks you're sick.	He <u>thought</u> you were sick.
They find their keys.	They <u>found</u> their keys.
Mr. Parker says "yes."	Mr. Parker <u>said</u> "yes."
They lose the money.	The <u>lost</u> the money.
I wear jeans and a tee shirt.	I <u>wore</u> jeans and a tee shirt.
He puts milk in his coffee.	He <u>put</u> milk in his coffee.
They tell the teacher the answer.	The <u>told</u> the teacher the answer.
He sends a fax to our office.	He <u>sent</u> a fax to our office.
The girls swim at the beach.	The girls <u>swam</u> at the beach.
I can speak French.	I <u>could</u> speak French.
You must go to work.	You <u>had to</u> go to work.

4. didn't . . .

I talked with my mother.	I <u>didn't talk</u> with my father.
We went by car.	We <u>didn't go</u> by bus.
She paid with cash.	She <u>didn't pay</u> by check.
We answered the easy question.	We <u>didn't answer</u> the difficult question.
They read a good book.	They <u>didn't read</u> the newspaper.
He wrote a letter in Russian.	He <u>didn't write</u> it in English.
I drank some wine.	I <u>didn't drink</u> any beer.

5. Did . . . ?

Do you go to work every Monday?	Yes, I do.
<u>Did</u> you go to work this Monday?	Yes, I <u>did</u>.
<u>Did</u> you go to work on Sunday?	No, I <u>didn't</u>.
<u>Did</u> Maria call her brother or her sister last night?	Maria called her sister.

Who called last night?   Maria <u>did</u>.

Who <u>did</u> she call?   She called her sister.

6. ago

Today is Thursday. Tom arrived on Monday. He arrived three days <u>ago</u>.

George Washington was president more than two hundred years <u>ago</u>.

We lived in Los Angeles fifteen years <u>ago</u>.

EXERCISES

A. Who cooked this delicious dinner?
   (My friend)
   My friend cooked this delicious dinner.

1. Who went to the supermarket to get some vegetables? (I)

   _____.

2. Who delivered this package this morning? (The messenger)

   _____.

3. Who painted *The Sunflowers?* (Van Gogh)

   _____.

4. Who wrote *Crime and Punishment?*
   (Dostoevsky)

   _____.

5. Who spoke to the office supervisor?
   (Mr. Menendez)

   _____.

6. Who came to our house late last night?
   (A stranger)

   _____.

B. The boys play basketball in the park.
   The boys played basketball in the park.

1. I answer the phone.

   _____.

2. Natasha speaks Russian with her friends
   from Moscow.

   _____.

3. We use the computers at the library to go
   on the Internet.

   _____.

4. They buy books on the Internet.

   _____.

5. He stays in a hotel in Chicago.

                                  _____.

6. I swim every morning.

    _____.

7. The salesperson takes my money.

    _____.

8. We have a very small apartment.

    _____.

C. You used the computer in my office.
Did you use the computer in my office?

1. He walked to work this morning.

    _____.

2. They ate breakfast together this morning.

    _____.

3. The engineer designed this bridge.

    _____.

4. Those men and women jogged in the park this afternoon.

    _____.

5. You cleaned your apartment last night.

    _____.

6. She understood the answer.

   _____.

7. We paid the phone bill.

   _____.

8. They got the fax that we sent.

   _____.

9. Your friend told them an interesting story.

   _____.

10. Your stomach hurt yesterday.

    _____.

11. They left four hours ago.

    _____.

12. He ran from the hotel to the train station.

    _____.

🔑 *A. 1. I went to the supermarket to get some vegetables. 2. The messenger delivered this package this morning. 3. Van Gogh painted* The Sunflowers. *4. Dostoevsky wrote* Crime and Punishment. *5. Mr. Menendez spoke to the office supervisor.*

6. *A stranger came to our house late last night.*

B. 1. *I answered the phone.* 2. *Natasha spoke Russian with her friends from Moscow.* 3. *We used the computers at the library to go on the Internet.* 4. *They bought books on the Internet.* 5. *He stayed in a hotel in Chicago.* 6. *I swam every morning.* 7. *The salesperson took my money.* 8. *We had a very small apartment.*

C. 1. *Did he walk to work this morning?* 2. *Did they eat breakfast together this morning?* 3. *Did the engineer design this bridge?* 4. *Did those men and women jog in the park this afternoon?* 5. *Did you clean your apartment last night?* 6. *Did she understand the answer?* 7. *Did we pay the phone bill?* 8. *Did they get the fax that we sent?* 9. *Did your friend tell them an interesting story?* 10. *Did your stomach hurt yesterday?* 11. *Did they leave four hours ago?* 12. *Did he run from the hotel to the train station?*

I Haven't Seen You in a Long Time!

WORD STUDY

John works Monday, Tuesday, Wednesday, Thursday, and Friday every week.

Today is Wednesday.

Last week, John <u>worked</u> five days.

This week, John <u>has worked</u> only three days.

She <u>believes</u> in Santa Claus.

Last year, Michael lived in New York. Now he lives in Boston.

Michael <u>moved</u> to Boston from New York.

He <u>has lived</u> in Boston for eight months.

Kenji's plate was full, but now it is empty.

Kenji ate <u>everything</u> on his plate.

Don't believe <u>everything</u> that you hear!

Kenji sees Chikako.

Chikako sees Kenji.

They see <u>each other.</u>

✺ DIALOGUE

🎧 *John:* **Sue? Sue Reynolds? Is that you?**

Sue: **John Cooper! I can't believe it! I haven't seen you in a long time!**

John: **We haven't seen each other in, what, six, seven years?**

Sue: **Well, I moved to Boston. I haven't spoken to you since I left.**

John: **How have you been?**

Sue: **I've been great. I'm married now, and I have two children.**

John: **Congratulations! That's fantastic.**

Sue: **And you, John? Is there anyone special in your life?**

John: **No, I'm single, but I have a lot of great friends.**

Sue: **We should have dinner. I'd love to talk to you about everything that you've done since the last time we saw each other.**

John: **I'd love to do that, too. Here's my phone number. Call me, and we'll make plans.**

VOCABULARY

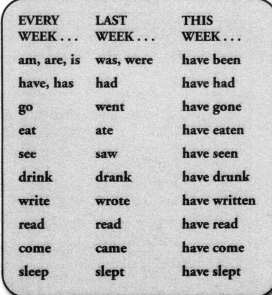

EVERY WEEK . . .	LAST WEEK . . .	THIS WEEK . . .
am, are, is	was, were	have been
have, has	had	have had
go	went	have gone
eat	ate	have eaten
see	saw	have seen
drink	drank	have drunk
write	wrote	have written
read	read	have read
come	came	have come
sleep	slept	have slept

wake	woke	have woken
buy	bought	have bought
sell	sold	have sold
take	took	have taken
give	gave	have given
speak	spoke	have spoken
hear	heard	have heard
get	got	have gotten
run	ran	have run
sit	sat	have sat
stand	stood	have stood
understand	understood	have under-stood
sing	sang	have sung
drive	drove	have driven
ride	rode	have ridden
catch	caught	have caught
throw	threw	have thrown
lie	lay	have lain
leave	left	have left
cost	cost	have cost

pay	paid	have paid
know	knew	have known
teach	taught	have taught
hurt	hurt	have hurt
make	made	have made
do	did	have done
feel	felt	have felt
think	thought	have thought
find	found	have found
say	said	have said
lose	lost	have lost
wear	wore	have worn
put	put	have put
tell	told	have told
send	sent	have sent
swim	swam	have swum
can	could	have been able to
must	had to	have had to

STRUCTURE

1. was / has been; slept / has slept

The children are in school every day of the week.

Today is Thursday.

SO . . .

The children <u>were</u> in school five days last week. (Last week is FINISHED.)

They <u>have been</u> in school four days this week. (This week is not finished . . .)

John goes to bed every night at 11:00, and he sleeps seven hours.

It's 3:00 in the morning now.

SO . . .

Last night John <u>slept</u> seven hours. (Last night is FINISHED.)

Tonight he <u>has slept</u> four hours. (Tonight is not finished . . .)

1st	2nd	3rd	4th	5th

The first one hasn't finished.

The second still hasn't finished.

The third was hasn't finished yet, either.

The fourth one has almost finished.

The fifth one has finished!

I'm reading a very interesting book, but I <u>haven't finished</u> it yet.

There are 300 pages in my book, but I <u>have read</u> only 200 pages.

The movie started at 7:30, and it ends at 9:00.

It's 8:30 now, so we <u>have seen</u> one hour of the movie.

The movie <u>hasn't ended</u> yet.

It's 4:00, and it started to rain at 2:00.

It <u>has rained</u> for two hours.

Yesterday, it <u>rained</u> all day.

2. -ed / -ed

FINISHED . . .	NOT FINISHED YET . . .
Ram talked to Amrita many times yesterday.	He has talked with her three times today.
They called their relatives in Mumbai.	They've called them many times this year.
Kenji walked to school yesterday.	He has walked every day this month.
Peter watched TV last night.	Tonight he has not watched TV yet.
Her plane arrived at 2:13.	His plane hasn't arrived yet.
They built the library in 1923.	They've built many buildings this year.

3. go / went / gone; eat / ate / eaten; speak / spoke / spoken

am, are, is	We have never <u>been</u> to Paris. Has she ever <u>been</u> there?
have, has	I've <u>had</u> too much cake already! I can't eat more!
go	They haven't <u>gone</u> to bed yet, but it's late.

eat	Have you <u>eaten</u> dinner yet tonight? Are you hungry?
see	I've already <u>seen</u> this movie, so I don't want to see it again.
drink	I don't want another cup of coffee. I haven't <u>drunk</u> my first cup yet.
write	We have <u>written</u> three post cards, but we must write four more.
read	Have you ever <u>read</u> *Moby Dick?* It's a great American book.
come	Has Kenji <u>come</u> home from school yet? It's already 4:00!
sleep	It's 5:00 in the morning! I'm tired! I haven't <u>slept</u> enough!
wake	Has your father <u>woken</u> up yet? No, he is still sleeping.
buy	Another new shirt? How many shirts have you <u>bought</u> today?
sell	The Morgans haven't <u>sold</u> their house yet, so they're still here.
take	Have you ever <u>taken</u> the subway in New York?

give	Your birthday was yesterday, so why haven't they <u>given</u> you a gift yet?
speak	I have an appointment with Dr. Johnson, but I haven't <u>spoken</u> to her yet.
hear	Have you <u>heard</u>? John got a new car!
get	John hasn't <u>gotten</u> a new car yet! He's going to get one tomorrow!
run	I've <u>run</u> too much, and now I'm very tired!
sit	He has just <u>sat</u> on the couch all evening. How boring!
stand	We've <u>stood</u> here for twenty minutes! Let's go!
understand	Could you say that again, please? I still haven't <u>understood</u>.
sing	Judy has never <u>sung</u> in front of hundreds of people!
drive	Have you ever <u>driven</u> from New York to California?
ride	This boy has never <u>ridden</u> a horse in his life!

catch	I still haven't <u>caught</u> the Frisbee. Throw it again!
throw	I've already <u>thrown</u> it a hundred times! I'm tired.
lie	It's 2:00, and I've <u>lain</u> on the beach since 10:00 this morning.
leave	Have they <u>left</u> yet? Close the door!
cost	No more clothes! It has already <u>cost</u> me too much money.
pay	Have you <u>paid</u> yet?
know	I've never <u>known</u> anyone from Thailand. It's nice to meet you!
teach	Our teacher has <u>taught</u> us a lot this year.
make	Have you <u>made</u> dinner yet? I'm hungry! I want to eat!
do	They haven't <u>done</u> their work yet.
feel	She's from Miami, so she's never <u>felt</u> so cold before.
think	Have you ever <u>thought</u> that he took the money?
find	I still haven't <u>found</u> my money.

say	I've never <u>said</u> that!
lose	Have you ever <u>lost</u> your wallet before?
wear	I've <u>worn</u> these pants three times this week!
put	Have you <u>put</u> your clothes in the closet yet?
tell	Has the teacher <u>told</u> them the answer yet?
send	We still haven't <u>sent</u> my sister the flowers for her birthday!
swim	I've <u>swum</u> in the Atlantic, but I have never <u>swum</u> in the Pacific.
can	It's late, and I still haven't <u>been able to</u> call my parents.
must	I haven't <u>had to</u> go to work in four days. I have time off.

3. since / for

It started to rain at 2:00.

It's 4:00 now.

It's rained <u>since</u> 2:00.

It's rained <u>for</u> two hours.

I moved to Boston in March.

It's November now.

I've lived in Boston <u>since</u> March.

I've lived in Boston <u>for</u> nine months.

I got home at 6:30.

It's 9:00 now.

I've been home <u>since</u> 6:30.

I've been home <u>for</u> two and a half hours.

EXERCISES

A. talk   talking   talked   _____

    talk   talking   talked   _have talked_

1. repair   _____   repaired   have repaired

2. go   going   _____   have gone

3. am/is/are   being   was/were   _____

4. _____   writing   wrote   have written

5. play   playing   _____   have played

6. see   seeing   _____   have seen

7. take   taking   _____   _____

8. work   _____   worked   _____

9. _____   sleeping   _____   _____

10. give   _____   _____   _____

B. She went to the movies three times last month. (this month)
She has gone to the movies three times this month.

1. We ate dinner last night. (tonight)

   _____.

2. They walked to work three times last week. (this week)

   _____.

3. I did the dishes last night. (tonight)

   _____.

4. We saw that movie last month. (this month)

   _____.

5. They were in London three times last year. (this year)

   _____.

6. I read for two hours last night. (tonight)

   _____.

7. I took the bus five times last week. (this week)

   _____.

8. The mail carrier delivered the mail yesterday. (today)

   _____.

C. 1. I _____ (go/am going/went) to the library every Saturday.

2. A famous architect _____ (designs/designed/has designed) our building in 1957.

3. The plane _____ (leaves/is leaving/has left) already.

4. The bus _____ (is getting/got/has gotten) here an hour ago.

5. We _____ (watch/are watching/have watched) TV now.

6. The plumber _____ (fixes/is fixing/fixed) the bathroom sink yesterday.

7. She _____ (gives/gave/has given) the money to the cashier a minute ago.

8. Last night I _____ (am reading/read/have read) for three hours.

9. They _____ (use/are using/have used) the computer at the library every Saturday.

10. The messenger _____ (delivers/is delivering/has delivered) a lot of packages already this morning.

11. They _____ (swim/are swimming/swam) in the ocean last month.

12. This professor _____ (teaches/is teaching/has taught) at the university for seven years.

13. The receptionist _____ (answers/is answering/has answering) the phone every day at the office.

14. Who _____ (paints/painted/has painted) the house last year?

A. 1. repairing, 2. went, 3. have been, 4. write, 5. played, 6. saw, 7. took, have taken, 8. working, have worked, 9. sleep, slept, have slept, 10. giving, gave, have given

B. 1. We've eaten dinner tonight. 2. They've walked to work three times this week. 3. I've done the dishes tonight. 4. We've seen that movie this month. 5. They've been in London three times this year. 6. I've read for two hours tonight. 7. I've

*taken the bus five times this week. 8. The mail
carrier has delivered the mail today.*

*C. 1. go, 2. designed, 3. has left, 4. got, 5. are
watching, 6. fixed, 7. gave, 8. read, 9. use, 10. has
delivered, 11. swam, 12. has taught, 13. answers,
14. painted*

Vocabulary